Darling the Window is on Fire

Darling the Window is on Fire

Written and Illustrated by

Wendy Hamilton

ZealAus
Publishing

Darling the Window is on Fire
Love and House Renovations

Copyright © 2019 by Wendy Hamilton
Illustrations © 2019 by Wendy Hamilton

www.zealauspublishing.com

All rights reserved.
No part of this book may be reproduced or transmitted in any form or by any means without written permission of the author.
Some names have been changed to protect identities.

ISBN: 978-1-925888-20-1 (e)
ISBN: 978-1-925888-31-7 (hc)
ISBN: 978-1-925888-18-8 (sc)

Contents

Family Genetics.................................. 1
Dogs in the House 8
My Dream Kitchen............................ 15
A Woman's Prerogative....................... 24
The Ideal Time? 32
Quality Control............................... 42
A Man of Action.............................. 50
Where Do We Start?.......................... 59
Good Missionary Training.................... 66
Moving Forward.............................. 74
The Language of Love. 78
Rat Troubles. 85
Old Putty and a Flax Bush.................... 95
Dresses, Colors, and Men. 103
Heat-Guns and a Dummy. 107
Darling the Window is on Fire. 116
A Good Neighbor............................ 125
Planes, Kids and a Wardrobe................. 132
I Told You So................................ 143
Unexpected Possibilities..................... 152
Renovations can be Romantic................ 159
About the Author 170
Other Books By Wendy Hamilton 171

Home Sweet Home

Wendy Hamilton

Family Genetics.

Like everyone else, I did not choose my genetics. Nobody consulted me when my DNA was constructed. If they had, I would have deleted the building gene. I could, however, water it down for my children. I decided to never marry a builder. This obsessive family-trait was horrible. I thought back to my teenage years. Endless building projects filled the weekends. It did not help Dad had no sons and firmly believed in equal rights.

"Women's liberation and equal rights stink!" I said to my sisters Antoinette and Rubella. "I bet Suffragettes never laid foundations for a concrete floor."

"Yeah, we're liberated into slavay," said Antoinette, lifting a shovel of rocks and dumping it into the trailer. "Other people buy fill but we dig for it."

"Actually, most people buy a finished house," I corrected. My sisters digested this a novel thought in silence.

"It's a pity this old quarry is on our land," said Rubella at length, as she levered out a big rock. "I hate this pickaxe, I've got blisters on blisters."

Darling the Window is on Fire

"I'll swap if you like?" I said, heaving my shovel over to her. "Thanks," said Rubella downing her tool.

I gazed enviously at Mum's little lightweight spade. "I wish Dad would buy us all a lady's spade," I said picking up the pickaxe.

"Seriously Wendy, would you really want a spade for your birthday?" asked Antoinette pulling a face as she dug.

My sister had a point. The desire was fleeting and only arose on Saturday mornings. What I wanted was a new bridle for my horse. Gifts were another reason not to marry a carpenter. While other women got roses, my mother got a lady's spade for her birthday. And last Christmas, her gift was a lightweight hammer.

"A good hammer is balanced," said Dad watching Mum unwrap her present. "Feel how nicely this one sits in your hand." He smiled complacently as Mum dutifully waved it about. When he thought she had got the feel of it sufficiently, he carried on, "as opposed to this rubbishy one." He handed her my present, a cheap hammer with a yellow handle.

"Mmmm," said Mum. She had no idea what he was talking about.

"Try them out girls," (Dad was on a roll) "feel the difference."

We all obediently held the hammers.

"No don't choke them!" Dad gasped as we grabbed them by their necks. "Hold them properly, down at the end," he said demonstrating.

We shifted our hands into the correct position hastily.

"See how this one balances nicely, but the cheap one drops heavily, that's the difference between a good and a bad hammer. Of course, the claw has to be good too…" A long-winded lecture followed.

Wendy Hamilton

"Remember the Christmas hammers?" I asked.

"How could we forget," giggled Antoinette.

"Don't dawdle, keep your mind on the job." Dad's voice cut our reminiscing short.

I swung the pickaxe and levered out a big brown rock. Despite his mild temperament, my father knew how to work us and had little consideration for our gender.

"That's another thing," I muttered to Antoinette under my breath, "I want to marry a male chauvinist. A man who thinks a woman should stay in the kitchen."

"I agree, I would love to be chained to the sink," nodded my sister, as we each heaved out a big rock.

"That will do," called Dad. The welcome words were long overdue. We threw our tools into the trailer and clambered up after them. The sharp, red rocks made a lumpy uncomfortable seat, but it was better than walking. The ride between the quarry and the house foundations was a pleasant reprieve. What a pity the distance was so short. When the car stopped, we eased ourselves stiffly over the tailboard and onto the ground.

"Don't start unloading yet. Wait until I string lines from the profiles," said Dad unexpectedly. He walked to the proposed concrete floor and stepped over the low wooden wall surrounding the perimeter. We meanwhile, snatched the opportunity to slump under a nearby tree.

"What are profiles?" asked Rubella.

"How can you live in this family and not know those pieces of wood in the corners, are profiles?"

"Dunno," shrugged Rubella. "What do they do?"

"You use them to make sure everything is level."

"The boxing around the sides makes it look like an empty paddling pool," commented Antoinette idly, as we watched our father weaving string back and forth across the expanse between the walls.

"What's boxing?" asked Rubella.

Now Antoinette was astounded at Rubella's ignorance.

"That wooden wall over there. The one that stops the concrete oozing everywhere," she said patronizingly, in what she hoped was a posh accent. She always used an English accent when she wanted to score over someone.

"You don't need to sound so high and mighty," said Rubella huffily.

"Yeah, it looks like the kid's pool at Mair Park," I cut in. "But when Dad has finished, it will look more like a tacky string picture."

"Ooo, you're right, remember those ugly ones we used to make at school?" said Antoinette, her voice returning to normal.

"I hope it takes a whole term for him to finish it," said Rubella, re-examining her blisters gingerly.

It was a vain hope and all too soon our break was over.

"Fill this area with metal," said Dad straightening up and pointing to a diagonal line. He pinged a taught string. "Put the big rocks at the bottom over by the sloping end where it needs more."

There were grumbles and moans as we reluctantly got to our feet. Only Mum, with her lady's spade, showed any keenness for the job.

"That looks good," he encouraged, as we trooped back and forth like a human conveyer belt. The rock-wall under the string rose steadily. Dad supervising, patted the top flat and applied his ruler to the shortening gap. "We need exactly three inches between the rock and the string," he said.

"Why exactly three?" I asked.

Wendy Hamilton

I went down the aisle confident I was eradicating the building gene.

Darling the Window is on Fire

"So, the concrete will be an even thickness," he answered looking serious. "We don't want it too thin."

"We don't want to pay for a thicker floor either," chipped in Mum. (Her Scottish blood abhorred unnecessary expense.)

The sun beat down as we worked and by lunchtime, we had a large horizontal X in place.

"That will do for the day," said Dad, as Mum lifted a picnic basket and a green cake tin out of the car.

Such sweet words. The afternoon was ours to do as we pleased. Perhaps Dad did have some consideration for our gender after all.

Weekend by weekend, we filled the triangular slices between the crossbeams of the X with rock and gravel. Then one day, an army of men and a big truck with a revolving belly came and poured the concrete.

Once the floor was down, building became fun. Us kids clambered about the framework and played our ukuleles as Dad hammered. From time to time we were roped in to hold up ceilings, lay paving-stones and plaster walls. When it came time for the drains, a man with a smart little digger, dug a huge moat around the house. Once the clay pipes were in, however, the fun stopped. Reluctantly we picked up shovels again, this time to push the dirt back. Dad did not see the point of using a digger twice when he had us.

Looking back, it seems as if my teenage years were filled with digging and building. By the time I was grown and Ian came courting, I knew how to plaster and paint walls, drive home nails, and the difference between a spade and a shovel. I also knew the eighth deadly sin was to use a screwdriver as a chisel, or a chisel as a screwdriver. Moreover, I could 'see' the framework behind a finished wall, and knew where things went when the toilet flushed.

I had not enjoyed gaining this knowledge.

"My father takes the motto Girls Can Do Anything far too literally," I said sourly to Ian. I liked this young man. His magnetic personality made me feel alive. Moreover, he was delightfully chauvinistic. Where my father said, "put your back into it, hold that beam higher!"

Ian said, "don't strain yourself Wend, I'll lift it for you."

I thought Ian's attitude was vastly superior to my father's. Ian had no idea what architraves or soffits were, he choked hammers and used screwdrivers as chisels. There were no builders in his family. There were farmers, nurses and a few factory workers, but no chippies thankfully. I went down the aisle serenely, confident I was eradicating the building gene. I was marrying an industrial chemist. The worst he could do was make soap or dynamite. Neither of which required my input. I looked forward to a life of leisurely weekends reading books in the sun.

So why have the last twenty-eight years of marriage been filled with building and renovation projects? The only possible explanation is genetics. There is no escaping DNA.

Darling the Window is on Fire

Dogs in the House

I stood in the hallway of our newly purchased house and breathed in deeply. It had the musty, old carpet smell that oozed potential!

Although I moaned like crazy as a kid, I was thankful for my fathers' training when Ian and I decided to buy a house. I needed the ability to see past the defects. The 1922 Californian Bungalow we chose, was shabby but had great bones. Scrim lined the walls, none of the door handles matched and the paint was peeling. To compensate, there were heavy beams on the ceiling, Redwood-doors, and a window seat. Unfortunately, all these features were reduced to nonentities by white paint. Mercifully, however, no paint defaced the square entrance. It was a pity the front door was not original. I opened it wide. The smell of potential was getting overpowering, I needed to let fresh air in, but when I tried to open the windows, I hit a glitch.

"Ian, there is something wrong with the windows," I called out to my husband. "I can't get them open."

Wendy Hamilton

"What do you mean you can't get them open?" He came briskly, swinging his new wrecking bar.

"Here, you try. I want to get this musty smell out of the house but the windows are stuck." I wriggled the catch open and pushed. Nothing happened. The window did not budge.

"You're not doing it right Wend, move out of the way." He threw his new toy on the window seat's squab.

I shifted my swollen belly to the side so he could get past me. It was irritating to be six months pregnant at such an exciting time. It clipped my wings somewhat. I would love to be taking a more active role in humping around furniture. In the background, I could hear our firstborn running through the empty rooms with the super-energy of a toddler. Beside me, Ian thumped and banged the window casement.

"You DOG!" he swore in frustration as it refused to yield. "How many of these dumb things are not opening?"

He tried all five windows around the window seat without success. On close investigation, we discovered every window of the house was a dog; except for the back bedroom, and one over the kitchen sink. At least the front and back door worked. I opened them wide and felt the fresh air stir through the house. From the sunroom (that never got sun) furious bashing reverberated through the walls, making the lampshades shudder. I heard a pop, and then silence.

"I got one open," shouted Ian victoriously. "It was a real DOG of a thing, but I got it open."

He stood beside the dangling window stroking his wrecking bar tenderly. "I couldn't have done it without this little beauty."

I looked at the stiff hinges of the vanquished window nervously.

"I hope we can get it closed," I muttered under my breath.

Darling the Window is on Fire

Meanwhile, my conquering hero ripped orange linoleum off the floor and threw it out the open window.

"Why would anyone put such ugly stuff over a solid timber floor?" I asked mystified.

"Maybe to hide the poker dots?" answered Ian, scratching a pink blob with the end of his wrecking bar.

"Fancy painting the floor blue, the dots are not even well done. They look like messy pink blotches." I pointed to dozens of faded cats prancing about the walls. "That wallpaper has got to come off too."

"Stand aside Wend, I'll do it."

"Just let me take the wrecking bar first Darls, you won't need it," I intervened hastily.

He reluctantly handed me his treasure before leaping at the walls with a great frenzy of scratching and tearing. I watched my husband's excited Terrier movements as he attacked the cats. Suddenly it occurred to me not all the dogs in the house were windows. We had not even shifted in, yet we were renovating. The old house had unleashed something primitive in Ian. He had stumbled upon his deep inner self. He had got in touch with the joy of demolition. When all the cats were lying crumpled and shredded on the floor, he wandered outside. Under the house were more delights.

"Come and have a look at this Wend!" His muffled voice sounded close to my feet. I waddled outside in time to see his head (festooned with cobwebs and dirt) emerge from a side trap door.

"Come under and see how rotten some of these old piles are."

"It might be a bit difficult!" I objected, eyeing the small opening.

"Oh yeah, I forgot about your condition, wait a minute."

Wendy Hamilton

He crawled out dragging the wrecking bar behind him and whisked ten baseboards off the side of the house slickly. There was no doubt about it, the man was naturally destructive. I remembered sadly, many teacups and several porcelain dolls. Why was I surprised?

"See how soft this is?" He held the wrecking bar like a Pro and jabbed the tool's tapered end deep into a pile.

I bent down awkwardly and peered at the exposed foundations.

"It's so rotten I can push this right through to the other side," he said demonstrating. "These old Totara stumps must be eighty years old. We will have to replace them before we do anything else."

I was disappointed. I knew he was right, but it would have been much more fun to paint the outside.

The front doorbell tinkled.

"Mum and Dad are here," I said, recognizing the voices. "We're round the side," I shouted down the path.

"How's it all going?" asked Mum, as she and Dad came around the corner. "Are you ready for the big shift tomorrow?"

"Nearly." I raised my voice and called through the back door, "Marie, Grandma, and Granddad are here!"

There was a thumping sound of small bare feet as Marie toddled out.

"How's my girl?" said Mum scooping her up. "I bought a thermos of tea and some scones for us all," she added glancing at me.

"Look how rotten these piles are Harold," said Ian poking at the foundations again.

"Come and have a cuppa when you have finished," I said to the men as I led the way inside.

Darling the Window is on Fire

Mum following me, lifted her picnic basket onto the sink bench and pulled out cups, and the green cake tin of my youth. Shortly after the tea was poured, the men arrived.

My father was very quiet as he munched scones. His face wore his thinking look. Eventually, he cleared his throat.

"Once you get settled, I'll show you how to deal with this little issue." His finger pointed down at the linoleum on the kitchen floor. As hideous as the seventies pattern was, I knew he was referring to the problem beneath it.

"That would be marvelous," I gushed. Without even realizing it my whole attitude to building projects had changed. The family gene was asserting itself. Like Ian, the house had unleashed something deep and primitive in me. Consequently, I was delighted when a few weeks later, Dad arrived with a huge mallet and a couple of bottle-jacks.

"Have you robbed a caveman Dad?"

"This is a present for Ian. I made it out of a small tree I felled."

My new attitude wavered as I looked at the long sapling handle intersecting a large stump. I shuddered at the thought of lifting it. I remembered Mum's lady's spade and hoped he had not made a smaller one for me.

"One whack with this and your old stumps will pop out like rotten teeth. Where's Ian? I want to show him how to use this."

"He's outside demolishing the woodshed," I sighed. "He went to move lumber and got side-tracked. I'm a bit worried. This love affair with the wrecking bar is getting out of hand. I saw him eyeing up the kitchen wall this morning."

"Don't worry, by the time he's had a few whacks with this, he'll have forgotten all about the wrecking bar," predicted my father confidently as he went out the back door.

Wendy Hamilton

Not for the first time, I marveled over the strange tastes of men. I did not find anything pleasant in digging, bashing or demolishing, but they seemed to relish it. Through the open window, I heard the men in my life reveling in the destructive power of Dad's gift. The house shuddered and a picture fell off the wall as Ian hit the foundations with gusto.

"Wow Harold, she's a beaut, that pile just popped out."

"You'll need to dig out the rotten stuff left in the ground, then you...." Their voices faded as I moved to the other end of the house.

For the rest of the day, bashing and digging noises filtered through the floor as I wandered about sorting china and finding places for pictures. I was glad that my condition barred me from participating in the delights below my feet. Basking in this happy thought, I pushed hard against the dog-of-a-door that usually scraped along the floor. To my surprise, it flew open and hit the wall with a loud bang.

"Hey what happened?" I yelled down at the floor. "The bedroom door is opening easily!"

"Try the windows," the muffled voice of my husband shouted back. I flicked the metal catch of a nearby window and gently pushed. It swung open without a hint of a fight. As I rushed about opening windows in delight, Ian joined me. He was covered in dirt and cobwebs and grinning widely. His hand still clutched his mighty mallet. Dad was right; the caveman tool had eclipsed the wrecking bar.

"I never realized fixing old piles could be so exciting," I said.

"Yup," Ian agreed, "there is not a dog-of-a-window or door left in this house." He did a little victory dance. Unfortunately, his joy was cut short as the end of the mallet fell off its handle, and onto his foot.

Darling the Window is on Fire

"You DOG!" he barked hopping up and down on one leg like an excited Terrier.

"Well, no architectural dogs," I agreed kissing him.

Wendy Hamilton

My Dream Kitchen.

Fifteen is an awkward age and I was an awkward fifteen-year-old. I was not a child nor was I an adult, and I did not know what I wanted in life. One thing I did know, however, I wanted an Auntie Hilda house. It captured my heart from the very first time I crunched up her white shell path and stepped over the backdoor step. The little old Kauri cottage oozed charm from the chickens in the cottage garden, to the wrap-around veranda. There was something magical about the humped picket gate dwarfed by the overgrown rambling roses. The house grew out of the hill like a face edged in flowers, clothed in bush. Directly behind the kitchen, the ground rose steeply. A patch of grass ran up the hillside. Auntie had planted it in daffodils, and in spring it turned into a wall of yellow, rising far above the red brick chimney. It was an understatement to say the house had street appeal. Its picturesque charm attracted artists in droves. There were always paintings of Auntie Hilda's house at the Craft-Fair held annually in the community hall.

Darling the Window is on Fire

And yet, despite the house's outer charm, it was the kitchen that really stole my heart. There was something so warm and appealing about the native timber walls and ceiling. Unlike most pre-war kitchens, the walls were unpainted. The tongue-and-groove paneling glowed with the virgin richness of Kauri timber cut from the surrounding bush. Only the sloping ceiling was desecrated by paint.

"When we first built the house, I wanted the whole kitchen painted cream. But my husband wanted it left natural," said the spritely eighty-year-old, as she cut me a generous slice of caraway cake. "So, we came to an agreement. He could have the first fifteen years and I could have the rest. One day I suddenly realized his time was up, so I got out my paintbrush and started painting. However, when I finished the ceiling, I stopped because I realized I preferred the walls and cupboards natural."

"I'm so glad," I said patting the stripy cat on the rocking chair. "I love the dimness. It is so cool and restful."

Auntie smiled as she poured the tea. The whole district called her Auntie although she was related to none of her neighbors. She put the tea caddy back on the mantelpiece above coal range. The black monster looked homely. An assortment of cake tins sat neatly stacked on the drying rack above the oven. I looked at the stove, the rag rug on the floor, and the cat-picture pinned on the cupboard door. The cat exuded the naïve cuteness only a six-year-old can produce. Somehow, the timber walls, fireplace, wooden table, cat and a rocking chair, made a resting place for my heart. It was about as far from a modern kitchen as you could get. From that day on, I knew what my dream kitchen would look like.

And it did not look like this.

"This is not like Auntie Hilda's kitchen," I said to Ian.

Wendy Hamilton

"I hate that tatty wallpaper and I loathe Pinex, cheap woodfluff held together with glue. Rats can eat through that stuff."

"It has its uses," said Ian, "Pinex noticeboards are great."

"What use is a noticeboard on the ceiling? I'm not planning to pin anything on the roof."

"You could pin a big poster over the water stain," suggested Ian picking up his chainsaw manual.

"A water stain is ominous," I said ignoring his impractical suggestion. "I hope the roof is not leaking."

"Hmmm," said Ian vaguely. He was engrossed in the art of the blade sharpening.

"And why paint a chimney bright orange? I suppose they considered it fabulously funky in the seventies?

"Hmmm."

"Are you listening to me? I think I could go into labor and you would just sit there reading that thing."

"You said, why paint a chimney bright orange, I suppose they considered it fabulously funky in the seventies," he said in a monotone.

"How do you do that? I know you haven't heard a word I've said, but I can never catch you out!"

"Hmmm." He was back to monosyllables.

"They probably put that stupid little potbelly stove in there at the same time," I said looking at the offending item in the orange cavity. "I bet there was a proper wood range in there originally. It is the right shape for one. I hate how the legs of this stove splay out into the room. They don't even fit on the hearth. It can't be very safe just propped up on bricks like that. I bet it doesn't have a Council consent. And this is really tacky!"

I flicked the metal track around the outer edge of the chimney opening. My father would never use this to cover

Darling the Window is on Fire

the join between bricks and wallboard.

"Hmmm."

"Give me that thing," I said, grabbing the manual out of my husband's hand. "You're very boring. I'm getting jealous of your tools of mass destruction! I'd rather talk to a woman."

Ian snatched his manual back. "You can talk to my auntie; she is coming to see our new house."

"When?"

"Tomorrow."

"Why didn't you tell me before this?"

"I forgot," said Ian disappearing once again into the world of chainsaws.

Typical, you can't rely on a man to pass on a message, I thought frowning.

"I love the house but the back area is a disaster," I complained to Auntie Monica as I led her into the kitchen the next day. I left it to the end of the tour deliberately. "This is not my dream kitchen. It is ugly. Fancy choosing a red bench. I hate Formica at the best of times. Some cupboards don't close properly, and the doors under the sink aren't even real wood. I suppose they were revamped in the seventies too." I banged a cupboard door above the bench shut.

"It's quite a tidy kitchen for its age," said Monica diplomatically.

"I suppose," I agreed, filling the kettle with water and sliding it on the stove. I looked around critically, for a rundown old house, it was not too bad.

"The windows are nice," I conceded.

"Yes," agreed Monica. "The red and green glass across the top is pretty."

The kettle whistled. I lifted it and filled the teapot.

Wendy Hamilton

"Perhaps we should drink our tea in more congenial surroundings," I suggested as I popped it and two teacups on a tray.

"I've brought you a little something for the baby," said Monica, as she followed me into the lounge.

"I had a nice visit with Monica," I said to Ian later that evening, after I had put Marie to bed. "She bought me a hat and booties for the baby."

"Hmmm, that's nice."

He was reading the annoying chainsaw manual again. I sighed. This could be another evening of monologs and Hmmms.

The cupboard door swung open and I slammed it shut for the umpteenth time. Suddenly something caught my attention. There was a discrepancy between the front and back of the door. The front was smooth, but the back was vertical boards. I opened the door and peered carefully along the bottom edge. Something of value was sandwiched between a thin layer of hardboard and ugly green paint.

"Hey Ian, I think this cupboard is made out of tongue-and-groove. I wonder if there is tongue-and-groove under the ceiling and walls."

"Hmmm."

Drat that blooming book!

"D E M O L I T O N," I said slowly and distinctly.

He dropped the manual and leaped to his feet. "Where do you want me to start?"

"I thought that would get your attention. Try chipping a bit off the wall behind the kitchen door. Let's see if there really is anything interesting under it. But use a chisel, and gently, this is delicate demolition, I don't want a big hole if I'm wrong."

Darling the Window is on Fire

I leaned over Ian and watched intently as he crouched down and chipped away at the wall.

"Yes, yes, there really is something!" I squeaked, swaying with excitement as a green board appeared.

"You might be right," said Ian his eyes gleaming. He looked at me hopefully.

"OK Darls, you can rip all that top stuff off," I said giving him permission.

Fearing I might change my mind, Ian briskly skinned the outer surface of the wall. I meanwhile, dragged the debris out the back door. As we suspected, tongue-and-groove paneling was hidden behind the wallboard. It was exhilarating and I felt like we had discovered buried treasure. I hummed a happy tune and everything was bonza until Ian reached the top of the door.

"Hey Wend, we have a little problem," he called, a worried note in his voice.

I dumped my load of hardboard on the back porch and stuck my head round the kitchen door.

"What's the matter?" I asked coming in.

"The paneling stops at the top of the door. There's only sacking and boards above it," he said pointing at the problem.

I reached up and stuck two fingers in the gap between the two lowest boards. Unlike the smooth, vertical boards below, these boards were wide, rough-sawn and lay in a horizontal direction.

"Wow, feel the draft coming through these! They must have covered the top of the wall with scrim and wallpaper," I said fingering a fragment of sacking. "I hate scrim. It sags in wet weather and looks awful."

"Not as awful as this looks. Are you regretting it Wend?"

"No, we can wallboard above the door and finish it with

a dado rail. Carry on, and while you're at it, you might as well have a go at the ceiling, we need to investigate that water stain."

Ian took up his wrecking bar again and hacked a hole in the ceiling with gusto.

I ducked a snowfall of white Pinex awkwardly.

"Hey watch out," I cried twisting my face up. Suddenly I saw something that made my heart leap. "I can't believe it, there is an Auntie Hilda ceiling under there too! I shouted beaming. "Have a go at the wall above the chimney, see what's under there, it can't be worse than the boards above the door, and rip that metal track off!"

As soon as the words left my mouth, Ian lunged forward with the claw of the wrecking bar. Within minutes the wall was skinned, and the track lay in a twisted heap on the floor.

"Oops, this is not too good Wend," he said stopping short.

My mouth drooped as I looked at the short boards above the mouth of the chimney. Missing boards marred the wall like broken teeth. Cobwebs, wafted in and out of the black gaps, as a draft blew down the chimney-stack hidden behind them.

"I was wrong when I said couldn't be worse than the boards above the door," I admitted. "Still, I don't think it's as bad as it looks. It will be fairly easy to replace the broken bits, At least they are short."

"Are you regretting this now?"

"Noooo," I said in a preoccupied tone. "Something is missing." I stared at the green outline on the timber. "The paint stops short. What did it go around?"

Ian leaned on his wrecking bar and contemplated the wall. "I know," he said straightening up, "a fire surround

Darling the Window is on Fire

and a mantlepiece."

"Of course, I don't know how I didn't see it straight off. Fancy ripping out a fire surround. I bet it was lovely."

"The demolition supermarket has a stack of them for sale," said Ian scratching at the paint with the end of the wrecking bar. "There's plenty to pick from."

"I'll go shopping tomorrow," I said in excitement.

Ian raised his eyebrows, "Do you want me to carry on?"

"Absolutely, rip all the wallboard off the cupboards. And haul up the lino as well."

As debris flew about in increasing chaos, I imagined the room transformed into Auntie Hilda's kitchen. In my mind's eye, I saw natural timber walls, a fabulous fire surround, and a black iron stove. From there it was easy to visualize a rocking chair, tabby-cat, braided rug, and a scrubbed wooden table. While Ian skinned the cupboard doors, I baked an imaginary cake and put Auntie Hilda's tea caddy on the non-existent mantelpiece. By the time I swept up the last pile of rubble, the kitchen in my head was lovely.

Therefore, Monica's reaction caught me by surprise when she turned up unexpectedly a few days later.

"Oooo," she spluttered, throwing her hands up in surprise as she walked into the kitchen.

"It's not that bad," I said.

Monica slapped her hands over her face, her shoulders jiggled and she made small snuffling noises.

"Are you laughing or crying?" I asked scratching my head.

Monica did not answer, instead, she quietened down, spread her hands and peeped at the kitchen through her fingers.

"There is nothing to be frightened off," I reassured her.

Her shoulders jiggled as she resumed snuffling.

"It will look lovely when it is finished," I added optimistically. "I'm going to replace the potbelly with a proper woodstove. I'll put my rocking chair here and a braided rug will look wonderful once we get all the paint scraped off the floor. It's solid timber," I said thumping it with my heel.

Monica groaned and squeezed her fingers shut to block out the view. Despite my description of the glories to come, Monica did not see my Auntie Hilda kitchen.

I gazed up at the ceiling, around the walls, and down at my bulging stomach. Suddenly I saw her point of view. I looked like a giant turtle, in a seaweed dress, in a bombed-out war zone.

"Would you like a cup of tea?" I asked weakly. "I didn't make a caraway cake, but I have biscuits."

Monica's fingers opened wide once more, and her eyeballs swiveled around the carcass of the kitchen. I followed her gaze into the black holes by the chimney. It was a grim sight. When a draft blew tendrils of cobwebs into view, it all became too much. Monica's fingers slammed shut again. Not even the world's best diplomat could call it my kitchen's décor tidy.

"Oh no thanks," she shuddered "I need to go!"

"It is not a dream kitchen," I admitted slowly.

"Yes, it is," said Monica, the wind blew her words back as she rushed out, "it's a nightmare kitchen."

A Woman's Prerogative.

"No, I don't like it there after all," I said. "Move it to the other side of the couch."

"You've had the jolly box there three times!" flared Ian, "make up your mind.

My husband's temper was a volcano, not Pompeii, it was safer than Pompeii. His was a benign volcano, the type tourists climb. While violent eruptions were unknown, little fiery upheavals spluttered regularly. The tourists or I were never in danger, as both types of craters were harmless, the bubbling mud, however, made interesting snapshots if you were quick with the camera.

"It's a woman's prerogative to change her mind Darls," I reminded him unperturbed.

"It is a man's right to not be bossed about by his wife." His eyebrows jutted out and his tone was hot lava.

"Of course, it is, don't worry about shifting it again, I will do it myself." I waddled over to the sea-chest and pushed.

Wendy Hamilton

There was a scratching noise as it slid forward an inch.

"Get out of the way, you're not to lift anything!" said Ian muscling in. He gripped both sides of the heavy box and swung the trunk into position easily. "I hope this will be the last time!"

"Thank you so much, it looks lovely there," I said, stroking the wooden ribs on the lid. "Just think, my great, great grandma bought her best china to New Zealand in this old chest."

"Why didn't you like it there the first time I put it there," grumbled Ian, unmoved by trivialities.

"I have to try all the possibilities, to make sure it's the perfect spot. Now I am happy. Don't you think it looks nice there?"

"Whatever," said Ian gruffly.

I took his whatever to mean yes. I had a policy of interpreting 'whatever' favorably.

"You won't change your mind about the color for the kitchen ceiling, will you?" he growled as he carried a heavy bucket into the kitchen. "Because we can't return this paint."

"Of course not. Buttery cream is the perfect color, white is too stark. Besides, Auntie Hilda's ceiling was cream."

"Well if Auntie Hilda's ceiling was cream, that settles it," teased my little volcano. The heat from his voice evaporated and his face crinkled into a grin. He levered the lid off the bucket and stirred the thick paint.

"It's logical to do the ceiling first," I said spreading drop-sheets over the furniture, it won't matter if we drip paint on the floor.

"Or down the wall," agreed Ian stirring vigorously, "what's a few more drips. Do you think this is mixed enough?" he asked wiping his stick.

Darling the Window is on Fire

"Yeah, near enough, it's impossible to get every streak out of it," I said peering at the paint.

"I'll bring in the trestles," said Ian dropping the stick with a clatter.

While he humped trestles and planks inside, I ran my eyes around the room. We had been busy for the last couple of weeks and the kitchen was greatly improved. A new dado rail ran around the walls, tidily separating the wooden paneling from the smooth wallboard above. Moreover, the broken boards by the chimney were fixed. Nevertheless, we had a long way to go before we could invite Auntie Monica back. The fourth wall was going to be a real challenge.

"I don't know what to do about that fourth wall," I said, as Ian stumbled into the room carrying a heavy plank.

"Begin with what you know…"

"And when you have done that, you will know how to tackle the rest," I finished off laughing. "You're no good at imitation."

"I am so. Who was I imitating?"

"Dad of course."

"Huh, you knew. That proves my point," he said hoisting a trestle upright.

"No, it doesn't. I've heard Dad say that a million times," I said pretending to punch him on the arm.

"Hey watch it, help me get these things in place," he said spreading open the second trestle.

For the next few minutes, we humped scaffolding into lines across the room. When we were done, Ian climbed onto the plank, tilted his head back and started slapping paint on the ceiling. By the end of the day he was finished. The narrow boards looked fresh and yet…

"Pity how the light color accentuates the sag in the

ceiling. I didn't notice any sag while it was still that motley green color," I said folding my arms. It was not the right thing to say.

My husband stopped washing the brush and glared at me. "Are you saying you don't like it!" he said his eyebrows jutting out and his face going red. I could see the volcano was about to explode.

"No, no, it's fine, I was just commenting, that's all. It will look fantastic once I wallpaper. Especially if I run a pretty border above the dado line," I said hurriedly.

Ian admired his handiwork. "Yes, it has come up rather well," he agreed, the heat going out of him.

"Maybe we could start stripping paint off the walls this week," I said, scratching at the green walls with a butter knife.

"Yeah, that's a good idea," he said shaking the brush dry.

So, on Monday night we had an early dinner and got to work.

"I am glad Marie is in bed," said Ian painting stripper on the wall. "This stuff is terrible. I wouldn't want a toddler anywhere near here!"

"Heck no," I nodded pulling a face. "It's dangerous and it stinks, but it shouldn't be too hard to get off, I saw how to use it on a video at the store and it's easy." I tied a tea towel over my nose and the lower part of my face.

"You look ridiculous, like a highway robber about to hold up a stagecoach!"

"Ha, ha, thanks for that lovely compliment." I threw him a clean towel. "Get this on Zorro. I'll get some dust masks tomorrow."

"I don't know how long I can hack this, my nose is squashed," grumbled Ian tying it over his face. "And Zorro

Darling the Window is on Fire

wore his mask over his eyes not like this."

"Whatever, don't nit-pick," I said poking at the slimy wall with a knife. The surface was bubbling exactly as the video predicted. I slid a paint spatula under it and pushed. My tool made a track through the chemical mush like a snow plow, pushing the paint into sticky corrugations. So far so good. When I tried to lift it off the wall, however, the advertisement and reality parted company.

"Hey Ian, this is not coming off properly. It's like melted gum. Are you having any luck?

"YOU DOG!" erupted Ian.

"Obviously not." I waddled over and squinted at his efforts. Instead of a clean path of grained timber, (shown clearly on the video), there was a streaky green track.

"What are we going to do?" I wailed. "How the heck are we going to get this gunk off the wall before the morning?"

"It says water soluble, perhaps we could hose it off," said Ian scrutinizing the back of the tin quietly. Now that we had a real problem, my husband's crater had cooled into calmness. I, however, panicked.

"We can't use a hose inside; water will seep under the door and ruin the hall carpet. Besides, the new wallboard will go soggy!" I shrieked.

"We'll just have to scrape it off as best as we can and sponge it down," said Ian thoughtfully. His level head steadied me.

"That might work," I said biting my nails. I took a deep breath. "This is going to be a long, evening."

And indeed, it was. The next morning, I gazed at the wall in despair. It looked like it was painted with glue and rolled in lawnmower clippings.

"Why is the wall yucky?" asked Marie opening her eyes

wide as she toddled in. "Did a naughty monster do it?"

"No, no, there's no naughty monster here, Mummy and Daddy made the mess."

She gazed at me in confusion, and I knew she was thinking about her scribbles on the wall. Suddenly I wished I had not gone on about them so much.

"Sit up at the table and eat your breakfast," I said quickly.

"It smells horrible in here," said Marie toying with her cereal. "Can I eat this outside?"

"Good idea," I said helping her down. "Carry your plate with two hands and don't run." She wandered out while I opened the windows and doors wide. The fresh air blew through the house taking the worst of the stink with it. Although it smelled better, I was still worried. I pulled Doctor Kneebone's Guide to Complete Family Health out of the bookcase. As I opened it, a four-leaf clover fell onto my lap. It did not make me feel lucky, however. I flipped through the pages and forgotten forget-me-nots, looking for reassurance. I could not find anything about paint stripper fumes, and I hoped that was a good sign.

Marie and I spent most of the day outside. By the time Ian arrived home, the fumes had died down.

He burst into the kitchen waving a new scraper.

"I stopped at the hardware store on the way home, and look at this beast I found," he shouted. "See this whopping orange knob, it lets me put some grunt into it."

He dumped his laptop on the table before lunging at The Wall.

"Wow, look at her go! You little beauty," he crowed, as rubbery paint and wood shavings cascaded to the floor.

"Here, have a go Wend," he said generously stepping aside and handing me the scraper.

Darling the Window is on Fire

I scratched hard and a sprinkling of dust wafted down.

"That's no good! Ya need to get ya back into it, here give it to me."

He snatched his treasure back and once more a great fountain of debris streamed off the wall. My husband was not a model. He was more functional than ornamental. But as his sturdy arms pumped like pistons conquering that huge problem, I found him highly attractive. He was so undeniably masculine it was romantic. In no time the wall was free of paint.

Every evening for the next week, Ian stripped the walls, and when they were bare, we coated them with polyurethane.

"This is my dream come true," I said as we rolled up the drop sheets on the last evening. "The walls glow. Once we get the wallpaper on above the dado, it will look even better. Can you pull the rocking chair out of the attic, Darls?" I asked, "so I can pretend the room is done.

Ian rolled his eyes, but I was not fooled. I knew he was as excited as I was. He disappeared and returned with the chair.

"You've been waiting a long time for this moment," he said rolling out a braided rug and setting the chair down.

"I sure have, and it's almost perfect," I said slowly, rubbing my chin.

"Almost," barked Ian the blood rushing to his face.

I studied the room perplexed. I did not need wallpaper, a fire surround, or even the fourth wall fixed, to know how it would look finished. So why did the room fall short of my expectation? I turned the puzzle over in my mind as I made a cup of tea. Suddenly it hit me.

"Darls, you know the ceiling you painted the other week?"

"Yessss," he said, his eyebrows sticking out.

"I think it would be better stripped bare like the walls. In fact, I know it would be. If it were natural timber, it would be truly perfect. All the paint has to come off."

My volcanic husband erupted. "Women! This is the sea chest all over again."

"It is a woman's prerogative to change her mind," I reminded him, ignoring the lava.

"Yes, and it's a man's right not to be bossed by his wife."

"You're quite right, don't worry about it, you've done enough, I will do it myself."

I put down my tea, pushed a chair next to the sink bench and made as if to climb on it.

"Oh, get out of the way," said Ian snatching up the scraper. "You shouldn't be climbing in your condition. Just sit over there and keep me company."

I yielded to his masculine authority, picked up my teacup and eased myself into the rocking chair.

"You won't believe what my boss did today!" said Ian scraping vigorously.

"What?"

"Well, you remember yesterday when he......."

I jiggled the cushion into the small of my back and listened to Ian blow off steam about work, poking snippets of my day into small pauses. And as the evening mellowed into cozy companionship, we brainstormed solutions for the fourth wall and built castles in the air.

There were no candles and it did not fit the definition of romance, nevertheless, I found it romantic. Romance is more than candlelight dinners. Restaurants have their place, but often an evening in is nicer than an evening out.

Darling the Window is on Fire

The Ideal Time?

Having a baby seemed the ideal time to call a plumber, not before the midwife but shortly after. I eyed the kitchen fire as I cooked breakfast between contractions. My pregnant stomach was not the only potbelly in the room. A bulging stove oozed out of the chimney cavity. It was not the original Shacklock stove. A Shacklock has an oven and a small efficient firebox, unlike this hungry monster with only a hotplate. I closed my eyes as another contraction hit me. Even in labor, the potbelly stove dominated my mind. It bothered me the front legs overshot the hearth. Some Bright-Spark (probably the guy who took the range out) had wedged a brick under each foot to keep the stove level. The contraction passed, I opened my eyes and stirred the chicken to keep it from burning.

"Ian, I think you need to call the midwife. Tell Linley not to hurry but I think it is time."

"OK Wend." He wandered off. I heard him talking on the phone as I opened the yawning mouth of the potbelly and threw more wood into its greedy stomach.

"The kitchen is the logical place to have this baby," I thought aloud. "It's spacious and warm."

"Linley's coming straight away," said Ian as he re-entered the room.

"Oh, she doesn't need to rush," I said, "I hope I have got time to tidy up the house a bit. Here, you dish out breakfast for yourself and Marie while I………….." A pain, faint at first, gathered momentum rapidly. I dropped to my hands and knees and breathed slowly as it grew to a crescendo, before fading away again, "while I have a quick whisk around," I finished.

I waddled to our bedroom and made the bed neatly. The cane bassinet in the corner looked lovely with its white drapery. I should put a hot-water-bottle in it to warm it up, I thought dropping onto my hands and knees suddenly. Why did kneeling make contractions easier? I shut my eyes and rode the wave of pain. As it thinned into nothing, I opened my eyes, stood up and went into Marie's room. It took me longer than usual to pick out clean clothes. I suspect I am getting past doing much, I thought leaning on the dressing table. Ian will have to dress Marie. I laid her clothes on the bed and went into the kitchen to wash the dishes. Washing the dishes also took longer than usual. As I dried the last plate, a gigantic contraction sent me hastily to the floor.

Wow, these contractions are getting big. Just ride them and concentrate, I thought, blocking the sound of Marie's voice out. I closed my eyes and breathed calmly. Suddenly my inner world shattered when something big and taut squashed my nose.

"Look at my loon Mummy? When Gamma and Ganddad come, I'm gonna show them my pretty loon."

Darling the Window is on Fire

"IAN! It is time to ask my parents to come and take Marie," I hissed through gritted teeth. "And get that balloon out of my face!"

The next few hours were a blur of activity. Linley came running down the driveway, Mum and Dad whisked Marie away, and contractions came and went, came and went. Finally, it was all over.

"You have another girl," said Linley laying Hannah in my arms.

Everything was cleaned up, Linley had gone and I was snuggled in bed, by the time Mum and Dad arrived back with Marie.

"There's no doubt about it, having a baby at home makes life easy," I said to them, as we admired the new family member.

"Marie stood at the side of the bed, her nose close to the baby's face and sucked her thumb.

"What do you think about your new sister?" said Mum.

I expected my verbose child to let go with a stream of words but she just stood there, silently staring.

"She must be really impressed," I said as Ian picked her up and carried her off to bed. "Thanks for taking her out Mum and Dad."

"No problem," said Dad. "We will go now and let you rest."

"Are you sure Ian will look after you?" asked Mum anxiously.

"I'll be fine," I said confidently. "He has taken two weeks off. I felt I needed the extra week because looking after a toddler is so tiring."

"I hope he washes the dishes and remembers to feed you this time," said Mum, referring to the week Marie was born.

Wendy Hamilton

"I've told him he is not to clean the gutters or do any outdoor work. He is going to focus on running the house and looking after Marie. Two years of fatherhood has developed him. I think he will manage alright."

And he certainly did. This time around the gutters stayed messy and the dishes were washed. Moreover, he looked after Marie well and remembered to feed us both. By the fifth afternoon, the strain was getting to him. He staggered into our room and collapsed exhausted on the end of our bed.

"Wendy, you do a wonderful job." He said the words in a weak voice but with utter conviction. In the background, I could hear ominous tinkling noises and a little high-pitched voice singing.

"Do be do be do. Da be da be dah."

As my husband lay spread-eagled with weariness, a cheery little person popped into the room and perkily announced,

"I've been shaving."

I gasped and Ian groaned. Marie held his razer aloft, while blood rained from her lips like Frankenstein.

"The first aid kit is in the bathroom cabinet," I said helpfully.

As Ian stumbled out with Marie tucked under his armpit, I snuggled deep into bed, glad I did not have to deal with it. The nicks were minor, but the mess was not.

While Ian was cleaning, my thoughts turned to the potbelly stove. Recently we had, by good fortune, acquired a Shacklock stove. It sat outside the garage gathering rust.

"I've been thinking about it," I said as Ian slumped on the bed, "I'm feeling good, and you still have a week off work. Now is a great time to install the wood-range. It is silly to pay so much for firewood. Those Shacklock stoves are much more efficient. Besides, when will you have time off work again?"

Ian sat up and looked me in the eye. "You want to see the new fire surround in place."

I nodded. "A mantelpiece is such a feature, it was a real score getting that one from the Demolition Supermarket," I said, my face lighting up. "But seriously, it will be cheaper to run."

"Your right, I'll get some quotes to install it, tomorrow."

Plumber number one and two arrived the next day. They looked at the stove, peered into the orange cavity, wrote notes on a clipboard and went away. A few days later, a price appeared in the letterbox. Plumber number three, however, investigated the stove meticulously. We stood and watched while he hauled bits off and poked about.

"Why do you want this old thing?" said Graham morosely. "You've already got an electric stove and a microwave, why bother with a wood-range?"

"It's more energy efficient than the potbelly and it looks gorgeous," I said, rocking the baby gently in my arms.

"Huh, no accounting for taste!" he said, with no attempt to hide his disapproval. He pulled an enormous pipe wrench from his tool kit and wound a pipe off the wetback. "You'll have to clean all this out if you want hot water," he said, running his finger around the inside of the metal box. Little flakes of iron rained thickly onto the driveway as he scratched and prodded. "And, you realize this pipe is on the wrong side for your hot water cylinder?"

Ian and I looked at each other our faces drooping. The more the inspection progressed the more depressed we became, and the more hopeless the job seemed. I felt like

Wendy Hamilton

Pooh Bear trying to fly by holding onto the string of a helium balloon. Graham was Eeyore throwing darts at my dream. Finally, when it seemed hopeless, Ian asked,

"But could it be done?"

"Oh yes, it could be done, anything is possible, but why would you bother?" said Eeyore.

"That's all I need to know," said Ian his face lifting. "I'll have this sandblasted and then I'll give you a call."

Towards the end of maternity leave, the stove was ready. The wetback was fixed, the rust cleaned off and it was gloriously black. We admired it as Graham backed his pickup down the driveway.

"It is astonishing what a rub of blackening will do! I said to Ian. He nodded.

The truck squeaked to a halt.

"Hello Graham, this is an exciting day," I said beaming, as he slouched out of his truck.

"For some," he said, banging the door shut. He stomped around to the back and wrenched off the tarpaulin.

"Gidday," said Ian grabbing the gas cylinder Graham thrust at him. "I'm your apprentice for the day."

"Good, take this too." He threw Ian a long rubber tube.

I wanted to hang around, but it was cold and I could hear the baby crying.

"I'll leave you men to it," I said, going inside.

Throughout the morning, noises came from the kitchen. I lay in bed listening to the sounds of bashing, dragging, grunting and the occasional burst of laughter. From time to time, a jackhammer rocked the house. Why stay in hospital and miss all this fun? Occasionally, I left the sanctuary of my bedroom to check on progress. The backdoor was wide open and an Arctic-blast whistled up the hallway.

Darling the Window is on Fire

Even in labor the pot belly stove dominated my mind.

Wendy Hamilton

The men were busy. The potbelly was out and the Shacklock was inside. It sat weightily in the middle of the room.

"I bet that was heavy to lift."

"Yeah, even with all the moveable parts taken off," said Ian. He wiped his face. Despite the freezing wind, he was perspiring.

"Time to put the jug on," said Graham.

Our taciturn plumber was thawing out. His faint accent suggested British origins and I guessed he was a tea drinker.

"Tea?"

"Yes please."

I moved carefully towards the bench; tiptoeing through extension leads, rubber tubing, and copper pipes. Heavy welding equipment leaned against the crockery cupboard. Great, no cups! Never mind, there were three dirty ones left in the sink. I quickly washed them, blew cement dust off the tea caddy and fished out four tea bags.

"One for each person and one for the pot."

As I dropped them into the teapot, a ferocious din ripped through the house as the men attacked the chimney. I put a finger in one ear and extracted the cake tin from under a pile of screwdrivers. Shouting was futile so I waved the tin. A sudden silence descended as Graham and Ian downed the jackhammer and the spotlight, respectively.

"So is Ian a good apprentice?" I winked.

"Given time he might scrub up," Graham grinned.

"Hey, hey, I've got the cake so you have to be nice to me," said Ian holding the tin high in the air.

"Do you think you will get the stove in today?" I asked, pouring tea into three cups.

"Oh yes," Graham said confidently, "soon."

Darling the Window is on Fire

After cake, tea, and a few sandwiches that I managed to slap together, I wearily dropped the dirty dishes in the sink. I tired easily and I rejoiced the upheaval was almost over. As I sloped off to my bedroom. Marie wandered down the hallway pulling a string of plastic ducks.

"Come with me," I said snatching up a basket of blocks. "Don't get in Daddy and Graham's way." I settled her with the blocks in my room. There was so no point putting her down for an afternoon sleep, there was too much noise. I shut the door tightly and the noise dimmed slightly.

"Play with your blocks, the horrible noise will finish soon," I said optimistically.

Six hours later, Graham and Ian were still working.

This is an elastic soon, I thought sourly, it stretches forever. I glanced at the bedside clock, nearly seven! The hall was a wind-tunnel, Marie was bawling, the baby wailed, and dinner was impossible. Suddenly I regretted calling the plumber so soon after the midwife. I pulled the hood of my thermal ski jacket over my head, opened the door and stepped into the hallway. As I shuffled forward, leaning into the wind, I heard a loud burst of laughter. Somewhere between lunchtime and now, Graham and I had swapped personalities.

"Do you think you will be much longer?" I asked morosely.

"Nearly finished, we just have to pop on the loose bits."

There was a flurry of activity accompanied by loud rattles and bangs. I held back tears as I clambered through plumbing flotsam and jetsam. Perhaps I have postnatal depression, I thought sniffing.

"What do you think Wend?" crowed Ian puffing out his chest. "No, hang on a minute, turn around, don't look." There was a pause (pregnant with scuffling) as the jovial plumber and his jolly apprentice maneuvered the fire surround into place.

"Now look!"

I turned and my face lit up with joy. The Shacklock looked so right. It nestled in the chimney recess, a perfect fit. As Graham lugged his tools out and Ian cleaned up, I plopped a kettle on the hob and lit a fire. The flame kindled and roared softly as a draft sucked smoke up the flue. One more thing would make it perfect.

"How about I get takeaways?" said Ian reading my mind.

An hour later I sat in my rocking chair with my feet on the fender. Ian next to me stoked the fire. The house was warm, the kids were asleep and all the difficulties had melted away. Already I had forgotten the day's labor pains.

"You know," I said, plunging my fork into a pottle of Chinese takeaways, "putting the stove in today was a good idea."

"Yes," agreed my wonderful husband, as the kettle whistled. "Maternity leave is the ideal time to call the plumber."

Darling the Window is on Fire

Quality Control.

Both Ian and I were involved in quality control. During the week, he was concerned with the quality of cement, and in the weekend, I was concerned with the quality of house renovations.

"Did you use a plumb line and a level on those steps?" I asked frowning.

He glared at me and I sensed lava about to erupt.

"Was I supposed to?" he flared, his eyebrows jutting out.

"Of course, you can't build anything without either of those! I'm sorry, but that's too rough, you'll have to do them again."

He threw down his hammer in a temper and shot me a fiery glance. "It's all your fault, you were talking on the phone!"

"I know. I talked longer than I realized."

He frowned, "you always yack for ages when your sister calls. What do you talk about?"

It was an awkward question, so I did not answer.

Wendy Hamilton

"Get the wrecking bar," I said to distract him. His face brightened and he rushed off to the garage. While we definitely needed the wrecking bar, sending him for it was a blind. I did not want to be quizzed. My sister and I had been planning a surprise birthday party for him.

"It would be so fun Wend. We could invite his friends and workmates."

"Yes, that would be fun. Thirty is a milestone, and I'd like to have a party while you are in Whangarei. His birthday is Friday so how about we make it for next Saturday afternoon?"

"That would work for me," said Antoinette, "I don't go home until Sunday."

"OK then, we will make it definite."

Then, while Ian built the steps, Antoinette and I discussed the party. The conversation meandered along pleasantly until a roar and a loud DOG-expletive cut it short. Ian had hit his thumb with the hammer.

"Oops, I've gotta go, see you later," I said whacking down the phone.

"I think you will lose your thumbnail," I said, inspecting Ian's thumb. "It's very red, you must have hit it hard."

"I did rather," he said heroically. "These steps are a dog-of-a-thing to build."

That was when I noticed how shoddy they were, and we had our little tiff. Sending him off to find the wrecking bar was a stroke of brilliance. While Ian searched for his favorite tool, I sat on the steps and thought about the party. Pavlova and ice cream perhaps, and a big chocolate cake from the bakery… I had got as far as sausage rolls and pizza when Ian popped out of the garage. He clutched his treasure tenderly as he bustled back to me, his temper fully restored.

Darling the Window is on Fire

Ian's surprise party.

Wendy Hamilton

I smiled. My little volcano was dormant once more.

"Just sit there and keep me company Wend," he said happily, as he levered out nails.

His attitude towards woman and work was superior to my father's attitude. And, provided I kept off the phone and regularly plied the plumb line and level, we got things built pretty well. We were a good team. He did the heavy stuff like smashing out old concrete and nailing up beams. I did the fiddly bits like putting on skirting boards and puttying nail holes.

By the end of the weekend, the back-veranda steps were finished and looking good. If the weather stayed fine, I might get three coats of paint on them before his birthday. The boards on the front veranda were rotting and the steps needed replacing, but for now, they were all right. I would weed the garden and Ian could mow the lawn on Saturday morning. That would also keep him out of the house while Antoinette and I prepared the food. The plan worked well in theory. On the morning of the party, however, I struck a glitch.

"Please mow the lawn," I begged, eyeing the wrecking bar in my husband's hand.

"Nope, I've got something better to do. The back steps are so successful I'm going to rip all the decking off the front veranda and fix the steps."

My mouth dropped open and I turned pale green. While our building endeavors usually turned out well, the process was messy. I had another dreadful thought. I was not available for plumb line and level duty.

"No, no that is not a good idea." I stuttered. "The yard is very overgrown. Please mow the lawn and rake up the leaves."

Darling the Window is on Fire

"Waste of time Wend, it will need doing again next week, whereas the steps and the deck have long-term value," he said bustling off.

I picked up the phone and called my sister when he wasn't looking.

"What could I say, Antoinette, he was so right, he stumped me with my own logic?" I whispered quietly. "He's out there even as we speak, removing the front steps. It is appalling the difference it makes. The front entrance looks like a derelict old wharf. Especially as he's whipped the baseboards off. I know we have to replace them, but it's ugly. I can see all the piles."

My sister was not helpful.

"No, it's not funny, stop laughing! At least he doesn't suspect a thing. He didn't even see the extra food in the cupboards or fridge. I never have cream or sparkling grape juice in the fridge normally. Come around soon. I need help. You know cooking is my weak spot."

I hung up the phone and stared out the window in despair. The guests were due and my husband was filthy. His knees were brown circles, his armpits wet circles, and his hair bristled in sweaty spikes. A surprise party had drawbacks. All the surprises were happening to me and they were all bad. As yet, the party boy had received no surprises. Even when the guests started to arrive, he did not twig.

"Hello Jan, lovely to see you," he said throwing down a rotten baseboard.

"Happy birthday Ian," said Jan. She handed him a brightly wrapped present and a card.

"Fancy you remembering it was my birthday!" said Ian. The tone in his voice rose in astonishment. "Come inside for a cup of tea." He led the way around to the back door.

"Isn't this nice," he said coming into the kitchen. "Jan has remembered my birthday."

"How amazing," I said, winking at Jan.

"I'll make a cup of tea while you have a quick shower," I whispered to him, glad for an excuse to clean him up. "I've laid clean clothes on our bed, wear those." I raised my voice and spoke in normal tones. "Go and make yourself comfortable in the lounge Jan," I said as Ian departed. "Would you like tea or coffee?"

"Coffee please," said Jan before she disappeared down the hallway.

Antoinette arrived.

"How's it going?" she asked, putting an enormous cake on the table. "I see the front yard is a demolition site."

"Don't laugh, it's not funny," I snorted, breaking into laughter myself. "Jan has arrived, but Ian still hasn't twigged it's a party yet."

"Where is he?"

"In the shower, I've finally managed to get him to clean up," I said making a pot of coffee. "He didn't even find it suspicious I had his clothes laid out on the bed for him."

"He's not very observant."

"Over some things, he is," I said, thinking of the small eruptions that flared up over the unexpected. "I'm surprised he hasn't guessed."

"Let's not say anything, let's see how many guests arrive before he realizes it's a surprise party," giggled Antoinette.

"Ooo, that sounds fun," I agreed naughtily. "Go outside and direct the guests around the back? We don't want anyone to break their neck trying to get to the front door."

"Alright," said Antoinette grinning.

She disappeared and I took Jan her coffee. Shortly after,

Darling the Window is on Fire

a stream of people passed through the back door and into the kitchen. Meanwhile, Ian (clean and seated in the lounge) welcomed guests and opened presents.

"Isn't this a coincidence," he said jovially to the crowded room. "Fancy all my friends choosing to call on me today!"

I suppressed a smile, wandered into the lounge and passed around nuts and chips. The guests and I exchanged grins before I whisked back into the kitchen.

"Hello Zoe and Mitch, come in," I said, as a tall man and a dark-haired woman arrived. "Ian is in the lounge. But guess what, we have twenty people here, and he still hasn't guessed it is a surprise party!"

"Do you need some help?" asked Zoe giggling.

"I sure do, could you whip the cream," I said handing her a bowl and a bottle from the fridge.

"Of course," she said taking them.

More guests filed in and stayed to help get the food ready. Things were really starting to roll. Now there were two parties; the formal one in the lounge, and the informal one in the kitchen. Surprise parties were fun after all. At least this one was.

"How long should I let this go before I tell him?" I asked Antoinette when she came in. A huge roar of laughter erupted from the lounge. I slid the serving-hatch open an inch and peered in. My husband, the center of attention, sat surrounded by friends and presents.

"What a coincidence," he exclaimed, "all you people coming here on my birthday!"

I turned back to Antoinette. "I should tell him," I said moving towards the door.

"Not yet," she said catching my arm, "this is too much fun."

Wendy Hamilton

Another roar of laughter floated down the hallway.

"Do you think he would get it if I took in the cake?"

"Let's try it and see," said my sister gleefully.

As I walked into the crowded room, bearing a cake alight with thirty candles, it occurred to me, a man incapable of spotting a surprise party, had little hope of noticing a crooked step. I must always hold the plumb line and never talk on the phone when my husband was building.

A Man of Action.

"Watch the table, watch the table!" I cried out in alarm. Too late!

There was a clunk and a thud followed by loud bawling. I glanced at Marie's head and the table leg anxiously. As I had made both the table and the head, their wellbeing was of utmost importance. I experienced a short inward tussle, as my house-proud Scottish ancestry, rose up and insisted that the table deserved priority. I repressed the ignoble impulse, however, and checked for blood, not paint.

"Be careful going around the table!" I said to my howling daughter for the millionth time. "You've got to watch the corners."

I parted her strawberry-blond hair and searched about. Thankfully, there was no blood or head lice.

"You're alright." As I picked her up, my toe whacked against the wheel of her heavy doll's pram.

"This shouldn't be in here!" I said through gritted teeth. "I've told you and told you, don't bring the pram in here, there is not enough room."

Marie put her thumb in her mouth and looked at me with big owl eyes. I grabbed the pram with one hand and maneuvered it around in a jerky three-point turn. Then I trundled it out the kitchen and down the hallway. As I slid my daughter off my hip and stood her on the floor, I said:

"If you want to bring your baby into the kitchen, carry her, and watch out for the corners of the table"….. "And that goes for the cat too," I called over my shoulder as I headed back to the kitchen. I walked over to the table and peered closely at the wounded leg. There was a small dent in the golden timber and a white streak. Drat that cane hood. Those big old 1920s prams could pack a punch. I licked my thumb and rubbed at the line, scratching it gently with my nail until it disappeared. I suppose I could wrap some foam rubber around the table's corners, I thought. It's a pity the top is just above Marie's eye level. I shuddered at the ugliness of the idea.

The real problem was, the room was too small. No matter where we put the table, it interfered with the flow of movement. If I put it hard against the north wall, it obstructed the passageway to the door. If I moved it south, it cramped the bench area. West shoved it too close to the fire, and east against the pantry doors. Moreover, the fridge got in everyone's way. The fact was, there was nowhere for it to go.

"We've got to bite the bullet and do something about the fourth wall," I said to Ian later that night when the kids were in bed. "The solution is to remove half the wall and turn the laundry into a dining room. A huge room for a washing machine, tub, and a shower is ridiculous. It's only storing junk."

Darling the Window is on Fire

At the words 'remove half the wall,' my husband's eyes lit up. I doubted he heard 'dining room' or 'washing machine.' By the time I got to 'storing junk,' I was speaking to an open door, as Wreck-it-Ralph rushed to the garage for his favorite tool.

"I think we should start with this silly little thing," I said when he came back. I pointed to a wall the depth of a cupboard that jutted into the room a small distance from the bench.

Immediately a great flurry of activity erupted, and within in minutes, the wall lay dead at my feet like a cat's offering. There was no doubt about it, my husband was a man of action. I eyed the pantry speculatively.

"Hmmm, if we remove the pantry it will leave a big hole. Then we can imagine the wall gone." I said thoughtfully. "It should come out easily, it's not very well made."

As if I had pressed a start-button, Ian flung open the pantry's doors.

"Great idea, I'll have this sucker out in no time," he said, his face glowing with enthusiasm.

"Hang on! Wait until I shift the food!" I made a dash to restrain him before he swept all the cans and cereal packets off the shelves.

"OK, you do that while I wrench off the doors. He gave the left-hand door a wallop with the wrecking bar.

"No," I yelled ducking out of his way. "Use a screwdriver, I want to save the hinges."

"Oh, all right." He put the wrecking bar down reluctantly. "Where is a screwdriver?"

"In the tool kit."

He stumped out in search of it. While he was away, I stripped cans and packets off the top shelves and dumped them on the table. I worked quickly, glad of the reprieve. Unfortunately, Ian found the screwdriver easily. I was only half done by the time doors were off and chucked outside. He picked up his wrecking bar and rammed it in a strategic crack.

"Hang on, hold your horses," I yelled, as he violently shook the pantry. A can of peaches and two tins of tuna rolled over my foot.

He stopped levering and instead, explored the outside edge of the cabinet.

"I'm glad I started emptying from top to bottom," I said thinking of the dried lentils and red kidney beans. The idea of standing under a hailstorm of legumes was not pleasant.

"You dog!" swore Ian ignoring me. He had discovered hidden nails. "I'll need to cut these," he said poking at a nail.

"It might be easier to get at them from the other side of the wall," I said, lifting out a big bag of oats.

"Yeah," he said rushing off. Moments later a hacksaw blade shot through the narrow slit between the wall and the pantry. It sawed back and forth ferociously while I swept the last of the food from the bottom shelf. I was almost done when a man-made earthquake struck. The pantry parted company from the wall with ominous ease. We carried it into the laundry and leaned it against the washing machine.

"I can see why that came out so easily," I said pointing at several truncated studs in horror. "Someone has chainsawed a hole in the wall and just shoved it in. Dad would be horrified, that's a load-bearing wall!"

"He sure would," said Ian, reveling in the size of the hole. He grabbed the ironing board and danced around the room in a victory dance. I, however, did not feel so thrilled. The removal of the pantry revealed the housekeeping skeleton

Darling the Window is on Fire

behind it.

"Who in their right mind keeps a piano in a damp laundry, or a cot for that matter?" I muttered.

"You," said Ian twirling his thin partner.

"I didn't need an answer," I said huffily. My house-proud ancestors would be appalled. How could this level of slovenliness exist in a descendant of my mother and grandmother? While the overflowing laundry basket was almost acceptable in a laundry, it was totally unacceptable for the bike to be there.

"A big laundry is a disaster for me," I said to Ian as he threw his dancing partner down.

"So, you said, you're repeating yourself."

"Don't nit-pick," I said absently as a light bulb lit up my mind. I stared at a blue area on the floor. "This must have been a scullery once. See how the blue paint on the floor stops in a line along here, dividing the room into a small square and a large rectangle?"

Ian peered intensely at the floor. "You're right, this is where the wall used to be. I bet they painted the scullery at the same time as the sun room." He rubbed a pink poker-dot with his foot. "There must have been a third door somewhere."

He stuck his hand out the laundry door. Opposite, across the short entrance, was the kitchen. A small wall (presumably the end of the passage) stood between the two doors. Ian rapped his knuckles on the wall.

"This is tongue-and-groove matches the kitchen, and it stops at the top of the doors like the kitchen. But does it strike you as strange that this wall doesn't go to the ceiling like the others?"

"Your right. There is no logical reason for a shelf up

there."

I scratched my head and stared at the alcove. It was not big, about the width and depth of a fridge, and a perfect showcase for my doll house. Ian dragged a chair from the kitchen and climbed up to investigate.

"Be careful, the veranda posts and the shingles on the doll house are delicate," I warned. I held my breath as Ian poked about and estimated the size of the space with his arm.

"I wonder?" he said softly as he climbed back down.

I resumed breathing. Nothing was broken. "Wonder what?"

Ian did not answer. Instead, he barged into the kitchen and stared at the cavity below the alcove. In it stood an upright freezer. It was old, ugly, and left in the house by the previous owner.

"Wait, a minute!" I yelled discerning his intentions. "Move the table out of the way before you pull the freezer out!"

I ran into the laundry and snatched the empty basket off the top of the washing machine. Ian (ignoring me) rocked the freezer from side to side, inching it forward. While he worked, I rushed over to the table and swept cans into the basket.

"Where's the hammer gone Wend?" he barked. "This dog of a thing needs a whack before I can get the freezer out. I reckon they must have built around it."

"Where did you leave it last?" I asked stuffing spices and vitamin bottles into a supermarket bag.

"I don't know."

I thought of his builder's apron, hanging behind a bike wheel in the garage.

Darling the Window is on Fire

"Why don't you wear the builder's apron I bought you for Christmas? If you got into the habit of putting things back in it, you wouldn't lose things."

"Can't be bothered."

He stomped through the gaping hole in the fourth wall. I could hear him rattling about as I filled another bag with pasta and rice.

"Found it."

"Where was it?"

"On top of the piano."

Ian whacked the flimsy divide between the large pantry hole and the small freezer hole.

"That's got it," he said as the two holes merged into one. "Give me a hand with the freezer, Wend," he said, pushing the table hard against the stove.

I put my bag on the floor and together we 'walked' the freezer out of position by rocking it back and forth between us. When it was out, we peered into the cavity.

"Just as I thought, there used to be another door into the laundry," said Ian. "See the old door frame?"

"Yes," I squeaked, "that wall in the back entrance is a false end." I stared at it like a kid who has discovered a secret tunnel. "You know Darls," I said slowly, "an appliance recessed into the wall is not such a bad idea. Let's chuck away the old freezer and put our fridge in here." I jumped into the recess, "but instead of it facing this way, we could wall this side up and face it this way," I swiveled to the right and faced the shower.

"The shower has to come out if we do that," said Ian, his eyes gleaming.

"It will have to come out anyway. We can't have a shower in the dining room," I said pulling a face.

Wendy Hamilton

Ian raised his wrecking bar.

"But don't pull anything out yet," I intervened hastily. "Check there's enough room on the poker-dot patch for a shower, laundry tub, and a washing machine first."

"Yeah, there will be enough," said Ian keen to get on with ripping out the shower.

"Measure it to make sure," I said firmly.

"Where is the tape measure?"

"I don't know, where did you leave it?"

"It's in here somewhere," said Ian wandering around in circles.

As we hunted for the missing item, we brainstormed ideas. By the time the tape measure was located on top of the teapot, the laundry was remodeled. Well, in our heads anyway. The plan was to return the scullery wall to its original position. The laundry would merge with the kitchen as a dining area, while the scullery became a shower and laundry.

"We'll replace this window with two bigger ones," said Ian, dropping the tape and chalking windows on the wall. "The kitchen window is common for its era. We'll find matching ones, or at least, something similar."

I nodded, "the demolition supermarket has a good selection, and we can recycle the old window." I said picking up the tape so it would not get lost again.

"Yes," agreed Ian taking the tape from me and stretching it along the floor, "it can replace the scullery window and the scullery window can replace the toilet window."

"Good idea. I hate the toilet window. Louvers are so drafty."

"Yeah, there's no point recycling that one," agreed Ian, "I'll smash it up." He flicked the tape about and wrote down measurements in a small notebook.

"Will everything fit?" I asked anxiously.

"It's a tight squeeze, but it will work if we put the shower, tub and washing machine here, here and here," he said, pointing to three corners of the blue floorboards.

"That's marvelous," I said beaming.

The clock on the mantelpiece chimed nine times.

"Time to call it a night," said Ian his shoulders slumping. "I've got work in the morning."

"There's just one thing I'd like to do before we finish." I said, wheeling the bike into the corner, "Let's shove all the junk over here, and move the table into the new dining area. I want to imagine how it will look."

Ian's shoulders popped up. Without waiting, he rushed over to the table and hoisted one end aloft. There was a great avalanche, as boxes of cereal slid down and fell to the floor.

"Grab the other end Wend," he ordered, moving backward, dragging the table behind him.

I ran forward, grabbed the end and heaved it up.

"Watch the edge, watch the edge!" I cried out in alarm, as we staggered through the pantry hole.

TOO LATE!

A tremendous clunk jarred my arms and shook the house, as the table hit the wall with force.

"Aw no, I said be careful," I moaned, distressed by the new dent.

"Don't fuss, chill out," said Ian, as he banged my poor table down with a force that loosened the legs.

I thought of the little scratch made by Marie, and everything Scottish in me sighed. I could protect my furniture from a doll's pram, but not from a husband like that! A man of action has his drawbacks occasionally.

Wendy Hamilton

Where Do We Start?

Remodeling moved forward in squats and jerks, rather like the large frog I found under my bed when I was a child. The frog and I eyeballed each other for a long time. I wanted to throw it outside, but I could not bring myself to touch it. The vibrant green of its damp body and pulsating throat repelled me. I visualized my hand picking it up, but my fingers refused to cooperate.

The frog and I had reached an impasse.

He looked at me and I stared back at him.

He moved his throat and I swallowed.

His skin glistened and I broke out in a nervous sweat.

He jumped forwards and I jumped backward.

"DAD!" I croaked, "There is a frog under my bed!"

When you are ten, your father can fix anything.

That was nineteen years ago. I did not have a frog under my bed, but there was a renovation-toad in the house. Building was much harder and not half as fun as demolishing.

Darling the Window is on Fire

Moreover, there was far more crouching than leaps forward. I needed rescuing but was it not my father I croaked too.

"When are we going to finish the kitchen? Renovating a house in our spare time takes ages," I wailed to Ian as we stood in the unfinished dining area. "Everything has ground to a halt. We haven't even shifted the shower yet."

"We'll get around to it sometime," said Ian unperturbed. "We can't take the shower out until we find another place to store all the tools."

"And that's another thing. Now that winter is coming, we might need to use the bath," I said. "There is nothing like a good soak in a deep bath. It is a pain to have to remove tools before I can run the water."

"I'll shift everything when we get the garage re-clad," promised Ian.

"Yeah, and when will that be?" I said sourly.

"You're unusually grumpy. You normally don't mind the muddle of renovations."

"I don't mind them when they are progressing," I explained. "It is when they grind to a halt for months on end that I get fed up. We still haven't got the table out of the kitchen, and the fridge, shoved against the fourth wall, is hard to get into."

"We need it there to hold the plywood in place. You'd be the first to object if there was no wall between the shower and the kitchen."

"Well yes, it has to stay there until the shower is shifted," I agreed, feeling we were talking in circles.

"Don't worry about it Wend, hang-loose." My husband crossed his eyes, bent his elbows and knees, and shook his hands goofily.

"I wish we could get the windows in," I said refusing to

be distracted. "And that goofy hand waving is not making me less uptight. It never does," I snapped.

"I know how to make you feel better," said Ian rushing outside.

Where is that man going now? I wondered. A wrecking bar will not magically install windows. The dining-room-toad and I stared at each other. Two (recently purchased) 1920s windows leaned against the wall. In my mind's eye, I could 'see' imaginary-Ian cutting through the weatherboards, and nailing a strong lintel in place. Then what? My knowledge petered out. The problem was, there was a lot more to putting a window in than adding a lintel.

I skipped forward in my imagination.

The shower was demolished in a twinkling and the pantry gap was opened up properly. I was installing the shower in my imaginary laundry, when Ian whisked through the back door, waving a can of spray-paint.

"Come outside Wend, this will make you feel better."

I followed him and he led me to the back of the house.

"Ta-dar!" he said, pointing at the wall with a flourish.

"How does this help?" I croaked in the tone of an outraged bullfrog.

"I thought it would make you happy to see a window in the back wall."

"A real window, yes. But not a painted one. I can visualize quite well enough, without graffiti scrawled all over the walls. The neighbors will think some teenage hooligans have done this. A big white wall (like this used to be) is exactly what they go for."

"Hang loose Wend," said Ian, repeating his silly hand waving antics. "You won't see it once I cut the hole in the wall. Besides, we are going to paint the house anyway. Here

Darling the Window is on Fire

I'll help you perk up."

He pressed the trigger of the spray can, and four stick figures materialized on the wall. He painted a smile on the hairiest one and squirted a hand and five fingers onto the end of its emaciated arm.

"There you are, waving to the world from your new window. And here………" he swirled a big blob next to a small one, "is the cat," he blasted a stiff tail over the wobbly windowsill, "lying next to Marie and Hannah enjoying the sun. Now the whole family is looking out the window."

The shrill rings of the phone cut short my barrage of unflattering comments concerning my husband's artwork. I stomped inside and picked up the phone.

"Hi Wend," (it was Antoinette) "I'm shifting back to Whangarei."

"Really?"

"Yes really. I'm coming at the end of the month. Do you think I could stay with you until I get my own place?"

"Of course, you can."

For the next hour, my sister and I talked. When we had finished, I hung up the phone and went in search of Ian. I found him seated at his computer doing the accounts.

"Darls," I said sweetly.

"So, you have forgiven me," said Ian, sorting through receipts.

"Oh, that little thing, the picture was rather cute." I paused. "Antoinette's shifting back."

"Good for her," he said, typing numbers into a spreadsheet.

"She's got a job down the road and needs somewhere to stay," I said it carefully. It did not take much for the volcano to erupt. Like a hot-blooded horse, a plastic bag blowing about in the wind could catapult him into a state of excitement, if it was unexpected. This was big-time unexpected, but Vesuvius remained dormant. He visibly expanded as he benevolently said:

"Tell her she can stay as long as she needs to."

I kissed the top of his head. I should have guessed his reaction. He was one hundred percent reliable in crises or difficulties. He was always there for me and helped those around him.

"You really are a kind man."

"What is she going to do with all her furniture?" asked Ian, suddenly looking stricken. "It's not all coming here, is it? We don't have the room."

"Don't worry, Mum and Dad are going to store it in their garage," I reassured him.

For the rest of the week I cleared out the spare room, and at the end of the month, Antoinette arrived. She arrived with a suitcase, a crate of doll-molds and a kiln.

"I'll teach you how to make porcelain dolls, Wend, you'll love it," she said as we hoisted the kiln up the back steps and in through the back porch.

I eyed it dubiously as it came to rest in the kitchen. I did not doubt my sister's claim that I would love making dolls. Despite this, I was troubled. The kiln was as bulky as my electric oven.

"Where will we put it?" I asked perplexed.

"Hmm," murmured Ian, examining the large plug on the end of the kiln.

While he pondered, I opened the firebox of the Shacklock and poked more wood onto the embers.

"I think it takes the same voltage as the electric oven," he said at length.

Darling the Window is on Fire

He grabbed the top edges of the oven and rolled it into the middle of the room. "Yup, it looks like it will work."

He wrenched the oven's plug out of its socket.

"Help me push the kiln over here," he said.

All three of us leaned against the kiln. Its small wheels rumbled and squeaked as they trundled over the wooden floor. When we were close enough for the cord to reach, Ian plugged the kiln into the stove's socket.

"Perfect!" he said. "You know, this is about the same size as the electric oven. It would fit in this gap. We could stick the stove in the garage and………"

"ABSOLUTELY NOT!" I interrupted him. "I know I am not much of a cook, but you are not taking away my electric oven!"

"Why not Wend? You've got the woodstove and that's lit every day to heat the water. Plus, you bake the bread in it."

"That is beside the point. It's one thing to do something because you want to, and quite another because you have to. Anyway, it doesn't fit properly. It's hexagonal, not square. Grime will fall down those big gaps at the corners.

"Not if we put a board across the back. You wouldn't notice it much."

"I would notice it. And so would everyone else. I want visitors to say 'what a darling woodstove', not 'what is that weird thing by the sink?'

"Where are we going to put it then?" said Ian. There was a hint of seismic rumbling in his tone.

"Oops, I think I will go and unpack," said Antoinette picking up her suitcase and sidling out of the room.

A gust of wind suddenly blew the door shut with a loud bang, and the plywood 'wall' wobbled. I looked at it thoughtfully. It would be dreadful to be in the shower and have the wall fall over.

"The kiln can go next to the fridge," I said. "It will help to hold up the wall."

"Great idea," said Ian wrenching the plug out of the socket.

Together we pushed it into place. If the room was crowded before, now with the addition of the kiln, it was bursting. I really needed a bigger room. I thought of the toad hidden behind the plywood. I knew in my heart, the main reason it was not leaping forward, was we were stumped; there are times in life a woman still needs her dad.

I went outside and sprayed another stick figure on the wall.

"Come outside," I called to Ian, "I want to show you something.

"What do you want?" asked Ian popping out the door.

"This is your father-in-law showing you how to put in a window," I said pointing at a new picture on the wall. I sprayed a line over the hand of the hairiest stick figure. "And this is me phoning him for help."

"Whatever," shrugged Ian.

I shook my hands and made a goofy face. At last, I could 'hang loose.' Dad would know how to get the toad out of the house.

Good Missionary Training.

Saturday morning rolled around again. Happily, Dad had come to our rescue, and the graffiti on the back wall had morphed into real windows. I looked through them at our sad looking garage. Our old car had died. Dad's ancient concrete mixer had killed it. Thirteen miles hauling the cement-encrusted dinosaur up and down the Mount Tiger hills was enough.

"I'm too old for this kind of thing," it said to its self, and wisely turned up its tires and expired.

Unfortunately, it died in the middle of the road, which meant nail-biting stress getting it home. And once it was home, our troubles were not over.

"How on earth did you manage to get the car stuck in the garage? It's jammed in on a diagonal!"

Ian scratched his head. "Dunno, it just sort of happened."

I threw up my hands. "I can't see how we can ever get it out again."

Wendy Hamilton

Antoinette pulled a chair close to the kiln.

Darling the Window is on Fire

"I suppose we'll have to demolish the corner," said Ian brightening.

"In any other garage, this would be a disaster. As it is, it just hurries things along."

"Yes," agreed Ian sheepishly. "Though I wanted to re-clad the garage later rather than sooner."

"It's a big job but worth it," I said, making the best of the unavoidable. "Fibrolite gets so brittle when it's old. Marie rode into the wall and made another hole in it yesterday. It's pathetic when a small child on a tricycle can cause so much damage." I eyed the huge hole. "A car wouldn't make a hole that big in plywood."

"Re-cladding shouldn't be too hard," said Ian thoughtfully. "I don't think we'll need your father's help this time."

"Yeah. We can copy what's there. You two did a good job on the windows," I said stroking the sill. "Dad's a great teacher. Learning how to do something is so empowering. I can't wait until this room is finished and the junk is gone."

I took the electric drill off the piano and carried it into the bathroom. Ian picked up a hammer and followed me.

Antoinette stuck her head out of her bedroom. "Is the shower free?"

"Yes," I said depositing the drill in the bath. It sat at a drunken angle on top of the skill-saw and electric planer. "One of the cotton sheets over the windows has fallen down. I think the nail has dropped out again," I cautioned.

"Here take a hammer with you," Ian said handing her the one he was carrying. "Put it back in the bath when you are finished.".

My sister twitched her fluffy bathrobe more tightly around her and took the hammer gingerly between her thumb and index finger. She liked the finer things of life, and our Spartan way of living grated on her, as her childhood formerly had. No matter how hard she tried to reject it however, she had the building genetics. She might speak with a posh accent, but her DNA remembered quarrying rocks and riding in trailers.

She disappeared into the laundry and shortly after I heard hammering. Bang, bang, bang. The bangs were hard-hitting and professional. No tentative tapping or hammer choking could produce a noise like that. There was a short silence, and then the sound of running water, falling in a torrent behind the plywood wall. As I flicked on the electric jug, a bloodcurdling scream made me jump. Shortly after, Antoinette burst into the room tightly clutching her bathrobe, her bedraggled hair dripping wet.

"What's the matter?"

"Ooooh, it was HORRIBLE!"

"What was?"

"I turned on the water and waited until it was steaming before I stepped in. I had no idea mist meant the water was freezing cold!"

I smothered a laugh. "Well that's strange, I had a lovely hot shower last night." I looked around as the jug boiled. "There's the problem, Ian didn't bother to light the fire this morning." I poured hot water into a cup and dropped a tea bag in it. "You need to stoke the fire for a couple of hours to get a really good shower. I suppose the rest of us used up all the hot water," I said callously.

The ability to laugh at yourself is a wonderful quality. My princess sister started giggling.

"You two should hire yourselves out as missionary trainers."

Darling the Window is on Fire

"Yeah, we'll start on you," I said, pulling the tea bag out and handing her the cup. "Here, get this inside, it will help warm you up."

"I'm a lost cause, you'll never get me to Africa." She pulled a chair close to the kiln. "You're probably the only people in the world to dry clothes on a kiln."

"No point wasting heat," I said flipping stretch-n-grow suits over like pancakes on a hot griddle. "The kiln is a bit inconvenient in the middle of the room when it is on, but it makes everything nice and warm. I guess that's why Ian didn't light the fire this morning. How many more hours until my head is fired?" I asked changing the subject.

Antoinette took a sip of her tea. "I knew you would love doll making. They will need a few more hours yet, and it takes ages to cool down, so it will be tomorrow before we can unload the kiln."

"Ian!" I called, catching sight of my husband in the hallway. The kettle's boiled. "Do you want a cup of tea?"

"Be there in a minute. Do you know where the hammer is? I couldn't find it in the bath."

"You gave it to Antoinette."

"Oh, that's right, where did you put it, Antoinette?"

"I left it on the piano. My traumatic experience drove all thoughts of the hammer out of my head."

"What traumatic experience?"

"We didn't light the fire this morning and the water was freezing."

"Yes, and I leaped into it," grimaced my sister.

"Is that so?" said Ian his face splitting into a wide smile. Princess Antoinette doused with freezing water was a delightful idea. He whistled a tune as he bustled off, and shortly after, bangs and thumps came from the small room that housed the toilet.

"Only you two would use the bathroom as a tool kit," said Antoinette sipping tea genteelly. "Just as well the toilet is separate. Otherwise, the queue in the morning would include people waiting for power tools. I don't know how you live with only one toilet."

"The bath is not much use," I said, ignoring her dig. "Have you tried to fill up an old bath? The water's cold by the time it's full. Apparently, the plumbing's the problem. Galvanized iron flakes in the pipes or something. Besides, where else would we keep the tools now the garage is non-operational. Anyone could walk in through the corner and carry off…"

SMASH! An almighty crash cut short my words.

"YOU DOG!"

Antoinette and I jumped.

"What was that?" I yelled.

Ian poked his head sheepishly through the kitchen door.

"Ummmmm, I've broken the toilet Wend."

"What do you mean you've broken the toilet? How could anyone break a toilet?"

"I sort of dropped the hammer in it."

"Sort of dropped the hammer?"

"Yeah, I put it on top of the cistern and it fell off."

His downcast face brightened as a new thought hit him.

"Seeing as we have to call a plumber, I might as well demolish the shower. Graham can disconnect the old pipes while he's here."

He whisked into the bathroom and rattled about in the bath. "You might want to find somewhere else to store the tools, Wend," he said emerging with his wrecking bar, "we will need the bath tonight."

Darling the Window is on Fire

"How could anyone break a toilet?"

"Oh my," groaned Antoinette.
"No car."
"No shower."
"And now,"
"No toilet."

She stuck her little finger out as she took a sip of Lady Gray tea.

"Darhling," she drawled turning to me, "a mud hut in Africa is beginning to look like luxury."

Darling the Window is on Fire

Moving Forward.

Sometimes setbacks move things forward. The broken toilet catapulted us ahead. Leaking water and sewerage is to plumbers what blood and heart attacks are to paramedics. Before my head was fired and the kiln cool, Graham had been and gone, and all that remained of the crisis was his bill, (which was a crisis of an entirely different sort.)

"Give us a hand Wend," shouted Ian excitedly. There was a cacophony of smashing and bashing. "Open the window and chuck all this stuff out."

He poked a huge shard of waterproof walling at me. I lifted up the window catch and pushed. The casement resisted at the bottom, so I gave it a thump with the palm of my hand.

"This window needs easing," I said, as I heaved bits of our former shower onto the driveway. I bent to pick up the shower-rose and mixer.

"Keep those Wend, we might be able to reuse them."

I stuck them on top of the piano next to the hammer

and Marie's pull-a-long Buzzy-Bee while Ian levered up the shower tray. Suddenly there was a volcanic eruption and 'dogs' flowed like lava about the room.

"There's a great whopping concrete base under this thing," he roared, flaring up at the unexpected.

I looked in consternation at the concrete pad he had unearthed. It sat flush with the floor so there was no way to whack flooring over top.

"I guess this is where the old copper was." I prized up the linoleum nearby and poked a screwdriver into the swollen chipboard underneath. "We have to replace this. Water has got in and we need timber to match the kitchen floor."

Ian bustled over and pulled up the lino.

"Ow," he said, banging his elbow on the wall. "We need more room." He disappeared into the kitchen, and the back of the fridge appeared as the plywood wall slid out of view. I grabbed the other end of the board as it scraped past me, and together, we carried our redundant wall out the back door.

For the rest of the day, we cleaned up demolition debris.

"That was one heck of a weekend," said Antoinette on Monday morning. "Is it always like this when Ian is home?"

The lid of the kiln was up and the kitchen table looked like a doll's hospital. She pulled a ceramic torso out of the kiln and put it beside six legs, and a book called The Five Languages of Love.

I picked up the book. "Only on good weekends. Sometimes nothing much happens. Putting things back together is much slower and tamer." I flicked through the pages. "This looks interesting."

"Yeah, I got it the other day. I thought it might contain useful information." She pulled a face. "Of course, I'll probably be a hundred before I meet Mr. Right."

Darling the Window is on Fire

"It will happen one day. Do you mind if I borrow this, I'd like to work out what Ian's language of love is?"

"Go for it," said Antoinette leaning over the edge of the kiln and digging deep.

"Ohhh, here's your head Wend," she said pulling a doll's head out. It's come out really good, apart from a little crack. But that's at the top and the hair will cover it.

She handed it to me and I held my head aloft, a smile spreading over my face.

"Yeah, that's me, a little cracked in the head for living like this," I said spreading my arms out like a showman.

Antoinette looked around. "It is rather grim," she said with a tinge of English accent.

"Only on that side of the beam," I said, pointing to the load-bearing beam separating the kitchen and the new dining room.

"When I get married, I'm not going to have an old house," said Antoinette going all haughty. She lifted her perfectly formed head out of the kiln. "I think a lifestyle of slogging every weekend and evening is so lowbrow."

"But the end result is so worthwhile. Look at my kitchen," I said pointing to the finished part of the room. "Doesn't it look lovely?"

"Well yes," admitted Antoinette softening a little. She lifted out a couple of mismatched arms. "But it takes a bit of doing to ignore that mess over there," she said, refusing to let me off the hook.

I stared into the dining area. An old piano, washing machine, and overflowing laundry basket leered at me. Worse still, was the gaping hole in the floor. When the wind blew, the musty scent of under-house and Tom-cats infused the air.

"The beam is the border between war and peace," said Antoinette, putting the arms next to the heads. "We are standing in peace and over there is war."

"Ian and I don't fight when we build. At least, we don't fight much."

"No, but you have to admit it looks like a bombsite."

I could see her point. The timber lining, wallpaper, and civilized order stopped abruptly at the border of the beam. I remembered Monica's horror over our kitchen and sighed.

"I hope Ian's Auntie doesn't visit us today," I said. "Although the kitchen has come a long way, I doubt she would see this new progress as a leap forward."

The Language of Love.

"Shut up Ian, I don't want to hear that," I said peevishly. "I want to read a bit more of my book before lights out. I'm trying to find out what your primary language of love is. You should read this after me."

"That's boring. Tell me Wend, what tune this is?"

"It's gross and I'm not playing that game."

Five primary love languages I read. Quality time. Oh yes, my husband is big on quality time. He is always seeking me out for companionship.

"Listen, fff, fff, fff, weee………. fff, fff, fff, weee," the snuffling noises broke my concentration.

"Shut up and let me read." I aimed a kick towards his side of the bed as he moved his face close to my ear.

Gift giving. I thought of my last Christmas present. Nope. A plastic dustpan and shovel didn't qualify as lavish gift giving.

"It's, 'Oh When the Saints Come Marching In.' Hear it?"

said Ian ignoring my protests. "Fff, fff, fff, weee……. fff, fff, fff, weee, oh when the saints……. come marching in."

"No, I don't! It doesn't sound like it at all. You can stop that nose whistling, it's ghastly, nothing at all to be proud of. Men are so gross. You don't hear women nose whistling, burping the alphabet or making rude noises with their armpits.

Ian put his finger on the side of his nose. "Listen to this one." "Fff, fff, sniff…fff, fff, sniff."

Acts of Service, a big tick in the YES box, I thought, tuning him out.

"Jingle Bells, did you get it! Try this next one. Fff, fff, weee, fff…fff, fff, weee, fff."

Physical touch, well he is a man, so of course, he is into physical touch.

"This Is the Day, hear it. Fff, fff, weee, sniff, this is the day, fff, fff, weee, sniff, this is the day, fff, fff, weee, sniff, that the Lord has made…"

"Why is it, as soon as I start reading you get annoying?" I said throwing down the Five Languages of Love. "You're like just like the cat. He always manages to sit on the exact newspaper article I'm reading." I flicked off the light. "It's time to go to sleep, anyway. You don't want a late night, you have work tomorrow," I said over the orchestra of sniffs, wheezes and whistles.

"Oh, all right Wend, but only if you guess this one. Fff, fff, weee, weee, fff, fff, weee, sniff."

"Amazing Grace," I said promptly.

"See you did know," crowed my husband triumphantly.

"I'll be pleased to have this hole covered in," I said on Tuesday evening. "It has been quite difficult keeping the kids from falling in."

Darling the Window is on Fire

I watched him work.

"The playpen around it should have kept them out," said Ian fitting floorboards over the rapidly diminishing hole.

"Yeah, to a certain extent. But it is easy for the girls to push it aside," I said.

"It's a good thing that they are generally obedient," said Ian laying down another board.

"Yes, I agreed. You did an amazing job smashing out that huge old copper base," I said changing the subject. "The concrete was so thick and hard."

He did not reply but the corners of his mouth lifted slightly, and he laid the next board down with an extra flourish.

I watched him work and pondered on Five Languages. Putting down a floor so your wife and children did not fall through a big hole, was definitely love. I was confident it qualified as an Act of Service.

"Do you like my new top?" I asked as a test.

"It's a bit red. Makes you look like a barn door."

I made a mental note. Scores zero for Encouraging Words. "Do you need a hand with anything?" I asked.

"No, just sit there and keep me company."

But ten out of ten for Quality Time.

"You know, we are not a very romantic couple are we." It was a statement, not a question.

"I can be romantic. I'll read Song of Solomon to you tonight," said Ian without skipping a beat.

"YUCK, don't you dare, that is worse than nose whistles or armpit noises!" I objected.

"What's wrong with it? It's the bible."

"You know perfectly well what's wrong with it, it is that soppy look you put on your face and the mincing tone of voice. And I don't know why Solomon considered it complimentary to say his beloved had a neck like a tower or teeth like a flock of sheep. All that suggests to me is the gallows and a lack of dental hygiene."

"Yes, I will read it to you," said Ian mischievously.

Too late, I remembered I should never have said 'don't you dare.'

"A man should read the bible to his wife. There are some really interesting bits in Song of Solomon," he said with a twinkle in his eye.

"I don't want to hear all the rude parts either."

"But it is the bible."

"I know, but I don't want you reading those bits to me. You can read Mathew, Luke, or John any time."

"Come over here and I will show you romantic," said Ian advancing playfully.

"Get away and finish the floor," I said throwing a tea towel at his head.

He stepped back quickly and stumbled against the wall.

"Hey look at this!" He said bending down. "This must have been behind the old shower." He plucked a small block of wood off the bottom plate of the newly exposed wall. "House built for Harold Brown in 1922. Dennis Christy one of the carpenters."

"Wow, that is so neat," I said thrilled. "Builders in the old days did this sort of thing. We did it when Dad built the Mount Tiger house." I peered at the date on the wood. "This is over eighty years old."

"Harold Brown," said Ian thoughtfully. "I'm sure that is the name of the first owner on our title deed. He was a grocer."

"It's a pity the plans were lost in the big fire at the council buildings. When Dad was a building inspector, he saw colleagues biffing out old plans because they had water stains on them."

"I suppose they weren't relevant anymore."

"Oh Ian, they could have donated them to a museum."

"Not everybody is into bungalows and villas like you Wend."

"Your right, Mum and Dad hate them. They worked hard to avoid a house like ours.

"I guess each generation has their own taste," said Ian. "I suppose our girls will love 1960s houses."

I shuddered, as I placed the precious block in pride of place on the mantelpiece.

For the rest of the week, I sanded back tongue-n-groove boards during the day, and in the evening Ian and I nailed them on the walls.

"The kitchen is coming along wonderfully," I said, one night towards the end of the week. I plumped up my pillow. "I can't believe how much we got done. I didn't think we'd get both the floor and the walls finished."

"It helped a lot that you stripped the paint off all the tongue-n-groove," said Ian getting into bed.

"Yeah, it was so much easier to sand the boards outside on the ground, than inside on the wall. Now all I have to do is polyurethane and wallpaper. That room is going to look so nice."

"Hmmm," murmured Ian as he picked up his bible.

I eyed The Five Languages of Love but left it closed on the nightstand. I did not want to remind my husband of my dare. He turned to the page headed The Eighth of August and continued with his scheduled reading.

What a relief.

No Song of Solomon,

Darling the Window is on Fire

No nose whistles,
No armpit noises,
No alphabet burping.
I smiled as he closed his Bible and turned off the light,
Everything was turning out very tame.

Suddenly, a red glowing triangle lit up the dark and floated like a UFO close to my eyeball.

"Give me those car keys!" I said snatching close to the weird object. "I'm sure the torch on the key ring was never intended to be the light in a nostril jack-o'-lantern!"

"Ha, ha, ha" chuckled my tormenting husband, delighted by my reaction.

We tussled, and the luminous nose briefly disappeared, only to re-emerge as I lost the battle.

The author of Five Languages of Love has some great things to say about love, but (bless his heart) he has missed one. The sixth language of love is teasing!

Wendy Hamilton

Rat Troubles.

A large orange dumpster stood in the driveway.

"Goodbye old kitchen," said Ian, heaving a huge armload of building rubble up and over the edge of the bin.

"It's wonderful to see all this stuff go," I said throwing in a pantry door. All this junk has been an eye-sore for so long. "I wish we could have got rid of it quicker."

"It wasn't worth getting a Jumbo-bin in before this," said Ian, as we walked back to the rubbish pile at the side of the garage.

"I know. I'm just glad it is going now," I said pulling the other pantry door out of the heap.

Ian scooped up another enormous load of wallboard, and together we walked back to the dumpster. For the rest of the morning, we trailed back and forth along the driveway ferrying debris into the bin. By mid-afternoon, the only sign of the ugly pile was a damp spot and a few bits and bobs. I cleaned up the bits and bobs, while Ian mowed the lawn. As I swept the last bent nail into my dustpan, the neighbor

Darling the Window is on Fire

popped her head over the tall fence.

"Hello Marie," I said looking up. "You'll be pleased to see we have finally got around to clearing up this eye-sore."

"Yes, that's nice," said Marie looking less thrilled than I expected. "I hope we don't get rat troubles now."

"Why would we?" I asked surprised.

"All the homeless rats will be looking for another home," said Marie gloomily. "The weather is getting colder; I expect they will shift inside."

"Maybe there were no rats living in the pile," I said optimistically. "We didn't see any when we moved the stuff."

"Just because you don't see them, doesn't mean they are not there. A rubbish heap as big as that, will definitely house rats," said Marie morosely. "I'll be putting poison down and setting traps. If I were you, I'd do the same."

She stepped off the bottom rail of the fence and disappeared from view.

I looked around the yard anxiously. Rats were a new and unwelcome idea.

"I think we should put down rat poison," I said to Ian as he trundled the mower past me. He stopped nearby and tilted it onto its side.

"Why," he replied, picking up a stick.

"Marie reckons the rats from that pile will be looking for a new home, and we should put poison down."

"Nah," said Ian breezily as he scraped grass clippings off the blade. "I didn't see any rats."

"That does not mean they are not skulking about," I said nervously. "The weather is cooling down; they'll be looking for a winter home."

"I'll protect you if one comes inside," said Ian cockily.

"Yeah right, the same way you protected me from the one

in the chooks house, when we were courting," I answered sarcastically. "You rushed out and shut me in with the rat."

"I didn't rush out because of the rat," said Ian huffily. "I needed to get more cleaning supplies, and I did not shut you in with it, the wind blew the door closed."

"So that's your story and you're sticking to it."

"I don't know why you wanted to turn that chicken coop into a bedroom, anyway?" Ian skillfully shifted the conversation away from the rat.

"Antoinette and I wanted more independence."

"Yeah, but a chicken coop!"

"You make it sound like a rabbit hutch!" By now I had forgotten all about the rat. "It was the size of a small granny-flat and had a tile roof. My father never built anything flimsy, not even a chook's house."

"True," Ian admitted. "The yard looks nice without all that rubbish, doesn't it," he said changing the subject as he flicked the lawnmower back onto its wheels.

"It certainly does. How about you trim around the path while I tidy up the garden?"

"Right oh," said Ian, wheeling the mower into the garage.

By the time we were finished for the day, I had forgotten all about the rats. It was not until bedtime I remembered Marie's warning.

"What's that noise," I said lifting my head off the pillow.

"What noise?" said Ian huffily, "I was asleep."

"Shhh!" I was not worried about waking him. Ian fell off to sleep with wondrous ease.

"I can't hear anything. What are we listening for?"

"Rats. Listen, I think I heard them above our bed."

We lay there straining our ears. Sure enough, we could hear scuffling noises in the ceiling.

Darling the Window is on Fire

"Perhaps I should have set some traps," said Ian at last.

"Mum said we can get rat poison free from the City Council."

"I'll pick some up on the way home from work tomorrow," said Ian

True to his word, my husband came home the next day with rat poison. He laid it around the house, under the house, and in the attic. I went to bed hoping we had dealt with the problem. Unfortunately, the rats were wily, or the poison took time to take effect. Either way, our sleep for the next week was interrupted with scuffling and squeaking. It seemed as if a large colony of rats had relocated their entire community into the roof of our house.

On Saturday morning, after a restless night, I wandered bleary-eyed into the girl's bedroom and pulled back the curtains. Outside the rain poured down. Suddenly, something in the tree oposite the window caught my eye.

"Ian!" I shrieked, "There is a dead rat hanging from the Phoenix palm!"

I heard a sound of galloping, as my knight in shining armor thundered to my rescue. I breathed a sigh of relief. It was so good to have a man to deal with situations like this. He burst into the room, took one look at the rat, turned tail and scarpered!

"Where are you going?" I wailed stamping my foot. "Don't leave me alone with this rat too," I yelled, remembering the courtship-rat. "You're the man, do something!"

There was no answer.

"What is it Mummy?" asked Marie and Hannah sitting up in bed.

"A dead rat," I said shuddering.

"Oooo where?"

Wendy Hamilton

"Out the window. Where is your father?" I stuck my head through the door and yelled down the hallway. "What are you doing?" I paused and waited for his reply. In the silence, I heard him fossicking in our bedroom closet.

"Is it still there?" he yelled excitedly.

"It's dead. It's not going anywhere unless you move it!" I shouted sourly. "What are you doing?" I yelled again.

"Looking for something."

"What's Daddy looking for?" asked Hannah.

I pulled my head back into the girl's room. "I have no idea," I said in a tone of exasperation. "This is exactly what he did when we were courting," I added under my breath.

"What did Daddy do?" chipped in Marie, her big ears flapping.

"Left me by myself to deal with a rat," I said briefly. I thrust my head into the hallway again. "Looking for what?" I yelled in the direction of our bedroom.

There was a bang as the closet door slammed shut, and the sound of running feet.

"My camera," replied Ian roaring into the room. "This is so cool. I can try my new zoom lens." He fiddled about trying several lenses.

"This is not cool. It's horrible! This is not the time to take pictures!"

"How is it even hanging there?" Marie piped up, clambering out of bed for a better look.

"It looks like it's hanging from a long tusk," said Ian peering intently through the window.

"I didn't think rats had tusks," "Perwaps it is a long tooth," lisped Hannah, slipping out of bed and sidling up to the window.

"Whatever it is, it is weird," said Ian. "Pull the curtain

Darling the Window is on Fire

wide open Wend, so I can get a better angle." He stared through the camera aperture and clicked the button. "You little beauty!"

I had no illusions as to whom the compliment belonged.

"This is going to be a great photo!"

I shuddered. "You're not going to stick that in the photo album, are you?"

"Why not?"

I visualized the rat between Marie and Hannah in the baby albums.

"It's disgusting," I said with heat.

"No, it's not." He took several more photos. "That will do," he said finally.

"Now, will you deal with this horrible thing?"

"Of course." He threw his camera on the bed and galloped off. I picked it up and put the lens cap back on. "That man would lose his head if it were not screwed on," I said, as I crawled around the floor collecting all the other lenses and caps scattered about.

"How could Daddy lose his head?" asked Marie taking my words literally.

"It's just an expression," I said putting everything back into the camera bag. "It means Daddy loses lots of things."

"Oh, you mean his car keys and glasses," said Hannah.

"Yeah, something like that," I smiled.

I looked out the window expecting to see my gallant knight removing the rat from the tree. Nothing had changed, however. The rain still fell in long strings and the rat dangled like a hideous wall hanging. I was about to go and see what my knight was doing when he returned with a mop and bucket.

"What's that for?" I asked puzzled.

"Open the window wide Wend. I don't want to go out in all that rain."

"But you have to go outside to get it, there is no other way."

"Oh yes there is."

He opened the window, and I watched as he hooked the bucket over the handle of the mop, and carefully guided it out the window and under the rat. Then he jerked it up in scooping movements.

"What are you doing?" I asked with growing alarm.

"I'm going to scoop the rat into the bucket," he said, grunting with exertion as he tried repeatedly (and without success) to dislodge the rat.

"Oh no," I said appalled. "I don't want that thing coming into the house."

"It won't matter Wend, it's dead." He moved his hands to the end of the mop handle and gave another swipe at the rat. This time he managed to knock his target before almost dropping the mop.

"This is not going to work!" I objected.

"Yes, it will."

He rested his arms briefly on the windowsill, before 'fishing' again. On the fourth scoop, the rat wobbled and fell into the bucket with a dull thump.

Triumphantly, Ian hauled his prize in through the window. "Just look at the size of the thing!"

I backed away from him rapidly. "I don't want to, just get rid of it!"

"I'll put it on the back porch, and bury it when the rain stops."

"Alright." I was willing to agree to anything, so long as he took the rat outside.

Darling the Window is on Fire

"There's a dead rat hanging from the tree."

Wendy Hamilton

"In the meantime, let's find where they are getting in," he said, sliding the bucket off the mop handle. "Obviously, they are climbing up the tree and onto the hood over this window. Then they are going up the wall. Perhaps there is a gap under the eaves."

"That sounds likely," I nodded. "It's very possible."

"You let down the attic ladder," he called over his shoulder as he carried the bucket out.

I passed into the sunroom. A ladder lay suspended high above me. A nylon rope ran from the bottom rung to a large brass cleat on the wall. I unwound the rope and let the sleek braid slip smoothly through my hands. The end of the ladder lowered gently to the floor in a wide arc. I rattled it, and the hinges holding the ladder on the wall wriggled slightly.

"I must tighten those screws," I said aloud. I flicked on the light switch by the door, and light seeped through the small cracks between the boards on the ceiling. Despite dubious flooring, the attic made a great storeroom. A draft blew past me as my husband rushed up the ladder, mop in hand.

"What do you want that mop for?" I ask mystified.

"To bash the blighters if we see them." He banged the manhole open with the flat of his hand and propped the lid against the side of the attic wall. "Come on Wend."

I followed him reluctantly. Light pooled around the naked lightbulb hanging from the ridge-board. Around the perimeter of the roof, deep shadows lurked. My knight in shining armor led the way, picking his path carefully. One slip off the rafters or nogs meant a foot through the ceiling and lots of work. A dark shape scurried along the sloping eaves.

"THERE HE GOES!" Ian yelled waving his mop

Darling the Window is on Fire

furiously. "THE DOG, HE'S MOVING TOO FAST, I'LL TRY TO GET CLOSER!"

He squinted shortsightedly into the murky depths. Slivers of daylight leaked through the edge of the roof.

"I can't see properly; I need to get my glasses. Here Wend," he thrust the mop at me. "If he comes this way bash him hard."

I stood speechless with horror, clutching my flimsy weapon. Before I could utter a word of protest, my husband was down the ladder.

"But," I squeaked.

My protest was too late. Ian's head disappeared into the room below and the manhole cover slammed shut. I was alone and surrounded by a colony of lurking rats. A feeling of Deja vu descended upon me. As far as preparation for marriage went, ours was a very honest courtship.

Wendy Hamilton

Old Putty and a Flax Bush.

"The only thing worse than shabby paint on a vintage house is aluminum windows and false bricks." I picked at the flaky paint on window casement as I spoke. A chunk of hard old putty fell out, rattled over the sill and landed with a plop in a patch of lavender.

"Yeah," agreed Ian, opening the ladder and standing it in the garden under the window. "A sure way to spend a lot of money and devalue a property at the same time."

"It's a desecration to 'modernize' villas or bungalows. They are part of our heritage. You can't get them again once they are gone. Reproductions don't have the same feel about them," I said climbing the ladder. I peered intently at the edges of the windowpane. "Most of the putty has to come out before we can paint," I said ruefully. "It's all broken and shriveled. Pass me a scraper I don't want to trample on the garden too much."

"Don't fuss about the garden," said Ian handing me a

Darling the Window is on Fire

metal spatula, "by the time we have finished painting, it will all be flattened."

I inserted the scraper between the glass and the putty and levered. There was a satisfying ping, and the plants below shook, sending out a faint aromatic whiff.

"This stuff is easy to knock out, it's so loose," I said. "No wonder the windows leak when there is a storm. This is not sealing anything."

Ian did not answer.

I turned around and saw him staring at the flax bush speculatively. It was large and crowded against the curving shingles of the bow window.

"You can take that thing out…" I started to say. Without waiting for me to finish, Ian shot off. "I NEVER LIKED IT ANYWAY," I shouted to the dot in the distance.

A noise in the garden next door caught my attention.

"What's the emergency?" asked Gary our neighbor, as he parted the leaves of a pittosporum bush and leaned over the fence.

"Oh, Ian wants another fix of demolition endorphins. Now that the kitchen is finished there's not so many things to bash."

"You've finished the kitchen at last," said Pippa, her head materializing through the leaves like a gigantic blossom. In the background, I could hear their young son making brrrrrrm, brrrrrrm noises as he played in a wooden crate.

"Finally!" I nodded. "You'll have to come over for a coffee and have a look."

"That would be nice," said Pippa lighting a cigarette.

"Gidday Ian, what are you up to mate? said Gary, as Ian reappeared, carrying a long metal bar, a huge machete, and a small chainsaw.

"How are ya doing Gary and Pippa?" I'm going to get rid of that dog of a flax bush. He dropped his load on the ground. "Just warning you, I'll be making a bit of noise." He said it as if he was delivering unusual information.

"Humph," said Gary, "there's been nothing but banging and thumping since you moved in."

"I suppose you're right," admitted Ian sheepishly. "How's business?" he asked changing the subject.

"Fairly quiet at the moment so I'm taking a break over Christmas while I can, once the end of March rolls around, I'll be flat out."

"The end of the financial year would be a busy time for an accountant," I chipped in. "Are you planning to go anywhere?"

"No, traveling with a toddler is hard work," said Pippa. She pointed her cigarette towards the happy noises behind her. The brrrrrm, brrrrrrrrms had changed into wheel rattles, punctuated by the occasional tinkle of a bike bell. "We are staying home. Gary has to paint around the windows, they are starting to flake."

"Yeah, ours too, you're lucky your house is brick and you only have to paint the windows. I'm not looking forward to painting the high bits of ours."

There was a sudden metallic crunch, followed by rowdy howling.

"Siggy's fallen off his bike again," said Pippa disappearing abruptly.

"Well, I'd better get on with taking out this flax bush," said Ian. "Catch you later."

Marie meandered around the corner of the house.

"Daddy can I have a car like Siggy's?" she asked, as she watched her father thump the heavy bar under the roots of

Darling the Window is on Fire

the bush.

"Ask your mother. You dog of a thing! Not you honey, these roots go down to China."

"What do you expect," I said, "it's a big bush. They say tree roots go as deep as the tree is tall, bushes might be the same."

"If that's the case, I will have to dig this as deep as a grave," said Ian ruefully.

I looked at the huge dry moat surrounding the plant and sighed. Nearby, Arum lilies lay trampled, their stems crushed, their creamy flowers bruised to transparency. My husband had spoken prophetically about the garden. It would be ruined long before we were done.

"Mummy, can I have a car like Siggy's one?" Marie piped up.

"You can make one out of a cardboard box. There is a big one in the garage," I said continuing to pick out putty.

"It's not the same." Marie swung on the ladder and my foothold wobbled.

"Don't swing on the ladder it's dangerous," I admonished, grabbing the window to steady myself. "A cardboard box is near-enough to a wooden crate."

"It's not that!" She held onto the side of the ladder and swung one leg.

"Siggy's car doesn't have any wheels you know?"

"Yes. But it has a real car seat and a real steering wheel."

The idea of derelict bits of a car in our backyard was horrid. "Ask his mother if you can play with him in his car one day. And take that putty out of your mouth!"

"I don't like him; he's got a funny name."

"He can't help his name. Parents call their children after people or things they find meaningful. Siggy is probably short for Sigmund Freud or (I thought of the smoking blossom) cigarette. If you don't want to go next door, put a chair in the box and use a plate for the steering wheel."

"It's not the saaaaame."

"Don't whine," I said exasperated, "go and play with Hannah I'm busy."

"I don't want to play in the sandpit, I'm bored."

"You can help me paint then."

I climbed down the ladder and went into the kitchen. Marie trailed after me and watched with interest as I took an empty honey pot out of the rubbish bin.

"What's that Mum?"

"It's a paint bucket," I said washing it briskly. I filled it with water and handed her a paintbrush. "Come on," I said leading the way outside again. "Go over there (away from Daddy) and 'paint' the wall."

As Marie skipped off, the front gate clicked.

"My, this is a hive of activity," said my mother coming down the path. "Hello Ian, that looks like a big job."

"Hello Anne," said Ian wiping his sweaty face with the back of his hand. Bits of dirt and lily juice smeared across his forehead.

"Grandma, Grandma," shouted Marie running up. "I'm painting the house."

Mum pretended to see fresh paint. "Oh, you are too, that looks lovely."

"I wanted a car like Siggy's but mummy won't let me have one, so I am painting the house instead."

"Never mind, painting is fun. Is Siggy walking yet?"

"Yes, he has legs."

Mum and I exchanged smiles over the top of Marie's head. "Come in and see the kitchen Mum, it's finally finished."

She followed me down the hallway and into the kitchen.

"It's so like Auntie's," she said looking around. "I would love her to see this. She has shifted into a home you know."

"She must miss her house and her chickens," I said, trying to imagine Auntie without them.

"I'm sure she does but they were getting beyond her. She is so spritely it is easy to forget she is nearly a hundred."

"What happened to Possy?"

"He died. Auntie found him dead in the woodshed. It is a blessing really, she couldn't have taken him with her, and cats don't re-home easily, especially one as old as Possy. The Forestry has bought the land and are going to tear down the old house."

"Oh, no, that place is a landmark; the district will not be the same without Auntie and her house," I said sadly. "Bring her round one day for a cup of tea. I would love to show her my kitchen. She has been my inspiration."

"I will, though I'm not sure how much she will be able to see, her eyesight is failing. This looks good over here." Mum leaped effortlessly from Auntie's failing eyesight to the positioning of the table.

"I know and see how tidy the fridge looks tucked in the wall."

"That is nice." Mum drew her eyebrows up and stressed the 'is' for emphasis. Speaking in italics and exclamation marks was a family trait. My family was not poker-faced or understated. "Have you done something different to the sink bench?"

"Yes," I said proudly. "I had a flash of genius. I took all those junky fake doors off the front and made new ones out of the left-over tongue-n-groove so they match the original cupboards."

"No!" (By which she meant yes.) "You girls are clever! You don't get your gifted hands from me. You and Antoinette sew and make quilts and I can't even thread a needle."

Suddenly the roar of a chainsaw shattered the peace.

"There goes Ian," I said hurrying up the hallway. "I'd better go out in case he chops off his leg. He is as fussy as an old woman over health and safety at work, but alarmingly casual at home."

The bright sunlight seemed glary after the dimness of the house. Stringy bits of roots and dirt were flicking in all directions. The dry moat was deeper, but the flax remained upright.

"Where are your protective glasses?" I bawled over the noise.

"Somewhere, couldn't be bothered looking for them," Ian yelled back. He switched off the chainsaw and dumped it on the ground. Then he thrust the metal bar deep under the bush and lent on it heavily. "Come and swing on this thing Wend." I stood close to him and together we heaved and swung. The bush wobbled and leaned to one side.

"It's coming, heave again Wend."

I leaned my stomach over the bar and swung like a kid on a jungle gym, while Ian jumped up and bought his full weight down on the end of the bar. There was a sucking, cracking noise as the bush yielded. I heard clapping.

"Well done, does this mean a bit of quiet for a while?" said Gary.

"Uh huh," nodded Ian. "We are just chipping out putty this afternoon,"

"What you want to do with an old house like that," said Gary critically, "is replace the wooden windows with aluminum ones, and cover the weatherboards with fake brick. A mate of mine had a wreck of a villa and he fixed it up with that stuff. It would add heaps of value to your place and save you all that painting."

I forced a smile onto my face. "Hmm," I murmured.

When it came to heritage houses, Gary was better at counting money, than spending money.

Wendy Hamilton

Dresses, Colors, and Men.

"White is so boring," I said biting my lip.

"You got married in white," objected Antoinette.

"I'm not talking about wedding dresses; I'm wondering what color to paint the house. Do you like this color?" I ringed a small square of butter-yellow paint and slid the chart across the table to my sister.

"Too yellow," said Antoinette dismissively.

I pulled it back, held it up to the light and squinted.

"Yeah. Three hundred colors and none of them seem right. I need inspiration."

"I like this one." Antoinette spun a Bride magazine around for me to see.

Now I was critical.

"The top is nice, but the skirt is a bit straight. I prefer the one you showed me a few minutes ago. It was more flared and had a ruffle around the bottom."

Antoinette fished another magazine out of the pile beside

Darling the Window is on Fire

her. "You mean this one?" She flipped through the pages and stabbed her finger on a vision-of-loveliness.

"Yeah, that's nice. If you put that skirt (finger stab) on the bottom of that top (another finger stab) it would be perfect.

"Hmmm," mused Antoinette staring at the two pages side-by-side.

"I wonder what color Mum and Dad will paint their beach house," I pondered, turning back to my chart.

"How about this gorgeous color," teased Antoinette, pointing to a garish blue.

"Oooooo yuck!"

"What's wrong with it Wend? Teal blue would match the sea. You could muralize mermaids all over the walls. Remember the caravan Mum had you muralize?"

"Puh, muralize! Is there such a word? I hate those huge sunflowers Mum got me to paint over it looked foul. They didn't make it look like a garden at all. It was hippy flower-power all over again."

"But she was so thrilled Wend. I'm sure she would love bright blue and think mermaids are jazzy," smirked Antoinette.

"I'm not painting 'jazzy' mermaids. That caravan is the last time I paint murals for Mum."

"Yeah right! You always do what Mum wants. Just be thankful that Mum is not into bathroom ornaments in the garden."

"Oooooo, I hate those things. Succulents growing in baths and toilet pans look disgusting. Why would anyone do that?"

"I suppose if you can't afford a fountain, a toilet is the next best thing. The cracked one in the junk pile is perfect for your front lawn."

Wendy Hamilton

I shot my sister a hard look. "Don't rub it in if you want to continue living here. I can't believe that man has broken two toilets!"

"He is getting skillful at it," said Antoinette. "I didn't hear him break the second one."

"No, he cracked it quietly with a screwdriver. It was a mistake letting him screw down the new one. Ian and porcelain are a disastrous combination." I glanced at my headless doll, lying forlornly in the mending basket.

"I don't know how you put up with him," sniffed Antoinette, deteriorating into haughtiness. "He would drive me nuts. You never need worry about us running off together, we would argue who went through the gate first."

I smiled because it was so true. It was a small miracle my sister and my husband had survived ten months under the same roof without a big argument.

"I love the way he bustles about and gets things done."

Antoinette looked down her nose. "The getting things done is alright, it's the breaking part that gets to me!"

"You can't separate the two," I laughed. "A man is not easily altered like a wedding dress pattern. You can't pick and choose his characteristics, he comes pre-packaged." I considered my sister's personality. "You'll probably marry a quiet man who has trouble making decisions."

"My husband won't need to make decisions, I can make them all," giggled my sister, climbing off her high horse. "My mouth defends an opinion before my brain knows I have one. I just want to meet the mystery man," she sighed. "All I can do is drool over wedding dresses. Waiting is hard, especially as thirty looms near. Sometimes I worry I'll miss out. None of the guys I have gone out with have been right."

"Why don't you make your wedding dress in faith? You

are good at heirloom sewing and you have plenty of spare time."

"That's an idea," sparkled Antoinette.

"Let's go to town and look at fabric," I said slapping the paint chart shut decisively.

"That sounds like fun. We could look for a pattern that combines both the skirt and top."

"Great idea," I said getting up from the table. I walked into the porch and pulled the folded stroller off the hook by the back door. "I need a walk. Besides, there are some nice old heritage houses down Shortland Street. Let's go that way so I can see what colors they are painted." I slipped the paint chart and a pen into my handbag and called the kids in from the sandpit. "Who knows, I might get inspired."

Heat-Guns and a Dummy.

"What is this?" roared Ian, knocking over a dressmaker's dummy one evening.

I picked up the fallen dummy and set it back on its stand. "Antoinette bought it today, she is going to make her wedding dress,"

Ian's eyebrows jutted out. "Isn't that jumping the gun a bit? She doesn't have a man."

"She is making it in faith."

"In faith for what?"

"That God will send her a husband."

"Oh." Ian glared at the dummy. "That red headless thing is ugly."

"I know, but it's useful." I draped a piece of white silk over the dummy's shoulder. "She has invited Sam around this evening."

"Who's Sam?"

"A guy she met at church the other day."

Darling the Window is on Fire

"Hmm." A glint entered Ian's eye. "If she gets married, she will leave my house. I hope he's keen."

I smothered a laugh. "That's nasty. She is no problem and she is helpful with the kids."

"I don't like it when she goes all hoity-toity."

I pulled a face and nodded. My eye fell on the paint chart. "I think I know the colors I want to paint the house."

Ian pushed dress pieces to the end of the couch before slumping down. "Oh yeah."

"Sage with olive around the windows and rust on the sills and baseboards."

"Whatever!"

The word exploded from his mouth. It was not a pretty 'whatever', and it was not a question. Ian's 'whatever' was like a New Zealand bush spider, big and ugly but completely benign.

I kissed him. "Oh, thank you, I knew you wouldn't care."

"I draw the line at pink paint and love-hearts. No self-respecting man allows hearts."

I avoided looking at the tiny hearts, poker-dotted all over the kitchen wallpaper. Below, large hearts ran around the dado like a chain of paper dolls. A woman can get away with much if she makes no fanfare.

"I'll never paint the house pink," I promised.

A red car pulled into the driveway.

I gasped. "Sam has arrived! ANTOINETTE, Sam is here."

Antoinette burst out of her room. "Oh no, he's early. He'll see the dress!"

I waved her away. "You meet him, we'll hide this." She nodded and checked her hair and make-up in the mirror.

"Quick, help me clear this up," I hissed to Ian, as footsteps ascended the front steps and clomped onto the veranda.

Ian catapulted out of his chair and together we scrabbled up pieces of wedding dress, then as Antoinette walked coolly towards the front door, we sprinted to our bedroom and leaped into its sanctuary, moments before the doorbell tinkled.

"That was too close for comfort," I whispered banging the door shut.

"I reckon," said Ian dumping fabric and pattern pieces onto our bed. Voices filtered through the wall as Antoinette welcomed Sam inside. "A wedding dress could kill a blossoming romance."

I slumped against the door. "We wouldn't want that."

"We certainly don't."

"How did last night go?" I asked my sister the next morning as she trailed into the kitchen for coffee. "He stayed a while. I could hear you chatting in the lounge long after Ian and I had gone to bed."

"He's good looking and has a great personality, but I don't know how interested he is in me. He does just enough to make me hopeful, but not enough to make me sure." She said it in her posh voice.

"It's early days yet."

Antoinette reverted to her normal accent. "We're going on a bike ride next Saturday. It's with a whole group from the hospital." Her nose rose and her top lip elongated. "Those physiotherapists and doctors are a rather intelligent group." She was English again. She sniffed suddenly.

"What's that funny smell?" Suspicion turned her back into a New Zealander. "Have the kids got into my curling tongs?"

"No, relax, it's Ian stripping paint. The back wall is

Darling the Window is on Fire

badly crazed and it all has to be removed."

"Was that the thumping and banging I heard early this morning? I thought it was a possum."

I moved towards the door. "I'm going to help him." "Did you see that I stuck the dummy and all the dress bits outside your bedroom?"

"Yeah, Ian fell over it and woke me up. Thanks for saving me last night. I would have died if Sam had seen that."

"No problem. Yell if you need a hand with anything. I'll be outside."

I wandered out. Ian was on the roof of the kitchen lean-to. He was wearing a dust mask and paint-splattered overalls. I tilted my head back and bawled out, "how's it going?

Ian switching off the heat gun. "Pretty good, this is easier than stripping the kitchen walls because it doesn't have to be perfect. We just need to get off all the loose and cracked stuff."

I scrambled up the ladder, crawled onto the roof, stood up gingerly and picked my way over to my husband. As I trod, my father's words reverberated in my head. "Never run on a roof, walk where the nails are, that is where it's strong."

I sidled up to Ian. "That's looking good, let me have a go."

He clicked off the heat-gun and handed it to me.

I pretended to blow-wave my hair. "Looks like a hairdryer."

"It would dehydrate your brains if you blasted that at your head."

"I reckon." I picked up a spatula, pointed the gun at the wall and pressed the ON button. It made a whirring sound and the smell of scorched paint filled the air. At first, nothing happened, then a blister formed. I pushed the spatula under the bubble and shredded a wide ribbon off the wall.

"This is fun," I beamed. "It would go faster if we worked together. Perhaps I should go and buy another heat gun."

"Good idea." Ian's voice was muffled by the mask. "Make sure you get a good brand. Don't buy junk."

"OK."

"And get a tarpaulin while you are at it. This old paint is lead-based. Nasty stuff. We don't want flakes in the soil."

I lowered myself over the side of the roof repeating, heat-gun, tarpaulin, heat-gun, tarpaulin. It was useless to make a list; the black hole in the bottom of my handbag devoured lists. Halfway down, however, I realized I did not have to take the kids with me. I bounced down the last six steps chanting under my breath, heat-gun, tarpaulin, ice cream, heat-gun, tarpaulin, ice cream.

The shop was close, it was possible to go there and return within twenty minutes. Nevertheless it was a full hour before I ambled around to the back of the house.

"Hello," I yelled.

Ian switched off the gun. "What took you so long?"

I fingered the popsicle stick in my pocket guiltily. He would not have minded me having a leisurely ice cream, but I did not want to admit it. The sun was fierce and his hot face covered with dust, smote me.

"Saturday morning is a busy time for hardware shops," I said lamely, starting to climb the ladder.

"I got two tarpaulins in case we wanted to work in different areas," I said throwing my purchases before me onto the roof.

He nodded. "Good thinking, I plugged another lead into the multi-box for you."

He pulled the new gun from its box and scrutinized the

Darling the Window is on Fire

packaging.

"Made-in-Taiwan," he read aloud. "Still junk but better than China."

"It's hard to find anything that's not made in China," I grumbled. "It is making shopping very difficult."

"Made in Australia!" crowed Ian brushing aside my problem. "See the triangle with the kangaroo." He paraded the logo on the corner of the tarpaulin like a philatelist discovering a rare stamp. "It would be even better if it had a kiwi in the triangle. Good for the economy."

The kitchen window opened and Antoinette's head popped out and swiveled skyward.

"WEND, DO YOU THINK YOU COULD GIVE ME A HAND FOR A MOMENT," she shouted up.

"OF COURSE," I called back, glad to escape the blistering heat of the roof.

"I need a hand adjusting the sleeves and the neck," said my sister, as I passed her head on the way down the ladder.

"Put it on, and I will be with you after I have washed my hands," I said easing myself onto the ground.

"What's the problem?" I said coming into her room.

My sister sat in her old jeans and a half-finished wedding bodice. "I've got to do this."

She handed me the instructions and pointed to a diagram.

"That's a weird construction."

"I know, but I think it is easy enough. I'll pull the elastic. Tell me when you think it looks right."

She pulled firmly and the right sleeve puffed, as the neckline tightened.

"Stop!" I commanded. "It looks good there." I pinned it in place. "OK, do the next one."

"Does that look even?"

Wendy Hamilton

That was too close for comfort.

Darling the Window is on Fire

"Just a bit more, that's it. You look gorgeous," I said ignoring the old jeans.

She tugged the elastic and the left sleeve puffed more fully.

"That will do," I said pinning it into place.

"It does look nice," said Antoinette preening herself before the mirror.

A mental image flashed into my mind.

"Huh, that top is the same style as Princess Diana's wedding dress."

Antoinette swiveled back and forth peering intently at her bodice. "You're right, I never noticed before."

"I like this pattern better though," I said, "because the skirt is not so overdone. Diana looked swamped in that huge veil."

A light knocking interrupted us.

I opened the door.

"Mummy, there is a man looking for Auntie Antoinette," said Marie.

"It's Sam!" said Antoinette in a panic. "Get me out of this!"

"Tell the man to go around the back and talk to Daddy. Auntie Antoinette will be out soon."

I slammed the door shut and ripped pins out of the bodice.

"You get dressed," I called over my shoulder as I dashed out for a clean trash bag.

"Shove everything in here," I said running back. Outside, small pattering footsteps followed by large firm ones passed along the path.

"Do I look tidy?" asked Antoinette stuffing the bodice into the bag.

"Fine, you go and say hello, I'll get rid of this."

"Thanks," she said patting her hair into place.

Hoisting the dummy under one arm and the bag under the other, I whisked down the hallway and into my bedroom. Meanwhile, at the other end of the house in my humble kitchen, The Princess welcomed her guest.

"Heloo Sam, doo come in. Would you lake tea or coffee?

I slunk out the front door and joined my peasant husband on the roof for a gloriously grubby afternoon. To each, their own. It was unlikely the suave young man in the kitchen, did anything as entertaining as nose whistling.

Darling the Window is on Fire.

"I don't know how you can live in such a cold house?" mimicked Ian in a high falsetto voice as he spread a tarpaulin under our bedroom window.

"Shhh, she'll hear you."

"I don't care!" Ian stuck his nose in the air and continued mimicking. "I just have to have sun and I hate verandas. I would never buy a house on a main road." He dropped his face and his voice returned to normal. "If she doesn't like it, she can find somewhere else to live."

He banged the ladder into the garden and jiggled it around in the dirt until it was level.

"You know she can't afford an apartment now that she is not working. She didn't realize that restaurant job had so much heavy lifting involved. She has nowhere else to go."

"Plug this in, would you?" He handed me the end of a long extension lead. "She could live with your parents."

"Huh. Antoinette and Mum, not likely! Lady Antoinette

is too much of a princess." I went inside, shoved the plug in the socket and switched the power on. "I would feel sorry for Mum," I said returning to the foot of the ladder.

"What about me? I can't move without falling over that stupid dummy, or the whopping kiln in the kitchen. Pass me up the heat gun. And every day the post brings more boxes to clutter the house."

"She needs to import molds for her doll-making classes," I reminded him, wrinkling my nose at the smell of blistering paint. "And she has her good side. She looks after the kids if I want to pop out for a while. Besides, you know you enjoy playing Monopoly or Bible Trivia in the evening. If she wasn't here, we wouldn't bother."

"I suppose so. I don't really have a problem with her staying. It just gets a bit much when she puts on that posh voice and turns all snobbish. The way she goes on, it sounds like we live in a slum's outhouse."

The burning smell intensified.

"I know, it gets to me too. She has been that way since we were children. If we get identical chairs, her chair is an antique while my chair is old junk. I just laugh or ignore it."

"I don't know how you can, it gets to me."

He rubbed the spatula up and down absentmindedly. A black mark appeared on the bare wood and a wisp of smoke wafted upwards.

"What about your parent's beach house? How long before it is finished? She is your father's responsibility, not mine."

The smoke developed into a spiral.

"It's coming along. Mum said they were putting the staircase in soon, and then Dad is going to start on the kitchen cupboards."

Darling the Window is on Fire

"Find out when it is liveable," said Ian, scratching at the window like a runner jogging on the spot.

A small flame flickered brightly and caught my eye.

"Darls, THE WINDOW IS ON FIRE!" I shrieked in alarm.

The heat gun flew one way and the ladder the other as Ian leaped to the ground.

"Turn the tap on full blast," he shouted as he scrambled to unravel the garden hose.

The noise and commotion as we doused the window, drew Antoinette from her bedroom.

"What's going on?" she asked, ambling out in her bathrobe with a towel wrapped around her wet hair.

"The window was on fire, but it is out now," I said wiping my brow.

"Here Wend, hold the hose and keep the water on the burned area," said Ian. "I'll climb up the ladder and check that it is really out."

"Could you shut the bedroom windows so the water won't get all over the place?" I asked my sister.

"Sure." She disappeared abruptly and shortly after the bedroom window banged shut.

"You can turn it off now," said Ian descending the ladder and retrieving the heat gun from the lavender patch. "It was only a surface burn luckily." He inspected the heat gun for water damage. "Good thing I threw this so far away. It is still dry."

He ascended the ladder again and pointed the gun at the wet window frame. I meanwhile, stood in the muddy garden and scratched loose paint off the shingles below. The drama had lightened Ian's mood, and we chatted companionably about paint and putty and garden plants as we worked. The sound of high heels clonking over the veranda, cut short Ian's opinion on cherry trees.

"Sam's taking me yachting with the hospital crowd today," said Antoinette wafting out. She wore a lavish wide-brimmed hat, sophisticated sunglasses and looked like she was off to the races. Sam's slick car pulled up at the gate. She swung a chic beach bag over her shoulder and waved as she floated down the front steps. "Enjoy your day. I'll think of you while I'm sunbathing. Ta ta." She left a whiff of perfume in her slipstream and then she was gone.

"Enjoy your day, I'll think of you while I'm sunbathing. Ta ta," mimicked Ian.

"Watch what you are doing," I cautioned, "the next fire might be serious."

"Yoo hoo."

I knew my mother's voice anywhere.

"Mum's here," I said before I turned my head.

"Hello Mum, good to see you."

"Hello Dear, I've got Auntie Hilda in the car, can I bring her in to see the kitchen?"

"I'd love you too," I said, turning off my heat-gun and putting it on the veranda rocking chair. I dropped my voice to a whisper. "You keep working Darls. They won't mind if you don't come in for a cuppa. I will send Marie out with a cold drink and a piece of cake for your morning tea."

Ian nodded. "That would be good, I don't want to stop, I'm on a roll. Find out how soon the beach house will be finished and suggest to your mother that your sister shifts into it."

"OK," I said over my shoulder as I hurried down the path to greet Auntie Hilda.

Mum was helping her out of the car as I scooted across

the footpath.

"Watch the curb Auntie," said Mum putting her hand under the elderly woman's elbow.

"Thank you Dear," said Auntie stepping out. For a hundred years old, Auntie was in very good condition.

"Here's Wendy," said Mum as they walked towards the house.

"Hello Dear," said Auntie giving me a kiss.

"Come in, come in. It's lovely to see you." I said. "Be careful, that bottom step is a bit wobbly."

Mum and I helped Auntie up the steps and ferried her down the hallway into the kitchen.

"What do you think of this?" said Mum. "Does this remind you of home?"

"Isn't it beautiful," said Auntie peering around. She stood in the center of the room dressed in sensible shoes and a neatly buttoned brown coat. A small felt hat with silk flowers and a piece of netting twisted around the crown sat on top of her smoke-gray curls.

"Can you see much?" asked Mum.

"Yes, yes, I can see the woodstove and the timber walls and the rocking chair. Oh, look! A tabby just like my poor Possy," she said, bending down to stroke the cat.

"Your kitchen has been my inspiration," I said as I put the kettle on to boil. "I wish I had some caraway seed cake to offer you."

"Come and sit over here," said Mum ushering Auntie to a chair at the table.

"Even the chairs look like mine," said Auntie with a shiny look about her eyes. She stroked the row of knobby spindles on the chair's back.

"Do you like my patchwork cat?" I asked pointing to a

quilt pinned to the wall.

Auntie peered in the direction I pointed. "I can't quite see it Dear."

"It doesn't matter. It is not as cute as the one Nicolas made for you."

"Dear little Nicolas. He was six when he made that for me. I used to take him for bush-walks and teach him all the names of the plants. He's at university now. And who are these little ones?" asked Auntie her attention diverted as Marie walked in, trailing Hannah in her wake. "What's your name, Dear?"

"I'm Marie and this is Hannah."

"Those are pretty names. How Old Are You?"

I'm four and Hannah is two and the cat is eight."

Marie could talk forever. While she chatted to Auntie, I drew Mum aside.

"How is the beach house getting on?" I asked biting my lip.

"Very well, we got the staircase in the other day. It was rather frightening. I had to sit on the top floor, catch it and hold it while your father maneuvered the bottom into place. I am glad that part is over and done with. It is so nice to have proper steps. I was sick of going up and down the ladder. Dad is starting the kitchen cupboards this week."

"He's not having a very restful retirement, is he?"

"Oh, he loves it and is glad he is still capable of building.

"Do you think Antoinette could move in there?" I asked quietly. "We have been happy to have her, but we didn't expect it to be a whole year. Ian is getting fed up."

"Of course, she can," said Mum instantly. "It's not right to saddle a young couple with that responsibility. You have your own children to think of.

Darling the Window is on Fire

We said she could come home but she wouldn't hear of it."

"I know, but she'd shift to the beach house. She can wallpaper it for you. She loves wallpapering."

"That's an idea. I'll talk to Dad about it."

Throughout the rest of the visit, I hugged the information to myself. As soon as I had waved them goodbye, I rushed over to Ian.

"The beach house is nearly finished, and Mum is going to talk to Dad about Antoinette shifting in," I said jubilantly.

"That is good news," said Ian smiling broadly. "Take the other end of the tarpaulin Wend, I've finished here."

I grabbed the corners and lifted.

Clumps of old paint rattled into the middle making the tarp sag. It reminded me of washing day and swinging the girls around in sheet hammocks for a special treat.

"I'm going this way," said Ian shuffling forward.

I tottered behind him trampling lavender regretfully. He halted under Antoinette's bedroom window where we dropped our burden and spread the corners wide.

"Ian, this old paint is surprisingly heavy. What are we going to do with it?"

"Bag it up in trash sacks. Because of its high lead content, it might have to go to the toxic waste area of the dump. I'll have to check it out." He retrieved the ladder while I dragged the extension cord and heat-guns round to the new worksite.

"That's good news about the beach house," repeated Ian setting the ladder up under the window.

"Isn't it just." I handed him the heat gun as he ascended. He pressed the on button. "How soon can she shift out? he asked, the hot nozzle getting perilously close to the glass.

"Maybe a couple of weeks."

Wendy Hamilton

"Isn't it beautiful?" said Auntie.

Darling the Window is on Fire

There was an ominous BANG and a long crack shot across the window pane.

"That is your sister's fault," roared Ian exploding. "I wouldn't have broken it if she didn't annoy me so much!"

Wendy Hamilton

A Good Neighbor.

"I can't believe your sister has finally gone!" said Ian several weeks later.

"The house seems so much bigger," I said twirling around the empty room. "Let's fix that broken window before we shift back the furniture. I don't want shards all over the bed. Do you think we need a glazier?"

"Nah, I'll just knock out the old glass, measure it up and bung in a new pane," said Ian as we went outside. "How hard can it be?"

A lot harder than we expected!

The professionals make it look easy; a thin strip of putty around the inner lip of the window frame for the glass to bed into, then a beveled layer of putty on top to hold the glass in and the water out. Simple in theory. So how did the glazier avoid this awful oozing mess?

I climbed up the wrong side of the A-frame ladder and scrutinized the window.

"Watch out," fussed Ian opposite me, "you're not

supposed to go up that way."

"It will be alright." I tapped the pane. "Perhaps if we squish the glass into the putty, some air bubbles with squeeze out."

Ian spread his hands and pushed until his fingertips flattened into white pressure points. The excess gloop on the inside of the pane spread without improving the problem.

I heaved a sigh of frustration. "It's no good, we'll have to try again. I'll push the glass out and you catch it." I scooted back inside and leaned against the glass.

"This is getting very greasy," said Ian pulling the bottom edge of the pane free with difficulty.

"The putty doesn't help," I said coming back outside. I scraped a sticky blob off with my fingernails. "It should be the consistency of bread dough, not hard lumps and oil. This is old. We should knead it more."

"You could be right," said Ian leaning the glass against the baseboards.

I scraped all the putty off the glass and gave half to Ian. We stood side by side squishing slimy lumps through our fingers.

"I loved this stuff when I was a toddler," I said.

"Whaaah," burst out Ian, thrusting gloopy hands close to my face.

"Ooooo," I squealed jumping back. "Naughty man!"

"Well you said you loved this stuff," said Ian unrepentantly.

"Yes, when I was a toddler and not in my face," I said pretending to smack him.

He smirked and we continued to squish putty companionably.

"I think it's soft enough now," I said after what seemed

to be a long time. "It's pliable and doesn't cling to my skin anymore." I dropped my rejuvenated clump back into the putty pot.

"I'll try less this time," said Ian rolling a ball into a long snake. "Pass me the butter knife." He spread the snake along the edge of the window frame, squashed it flat with the knife and pushed the glass into place. It was a bit better this time. "Where's that packet of thing-ummy-bobs?" he said looking around.

I fished about in my pocket and produced a small rectangular packet.

"Do you want me to get a screwdriver?" I asked handing it to him. "The guy in the hardware store said they were easy to use, just put the flat side against the glass and wriggle them in with a screwdriver."

"The knife will probably do," said Ian impatiently, "hand me a thing-ummy-bob."

I passed him a tiny silver triangle.

"It's a microscopic kite with feet," I joked.

Ian did not respond. His tongue protruded in concentration as he pushed the pointed end into the wooden frame and wriggled. There was a small ping.

"Blast! Where's it gone?"

"Somewhere in that bush, it's hopeless looking for it. Here," I handed him another one.

"Gently does it," said Ian. "You dog!" The knife flew out of his hand and he sucked the end of his finger, "it slipped right off."

"I'll get you a screwdriver," I said disappearing into the house. When I returned, Ian was in a state of excitement.

"Quick, quick, get up here or you'll miss it," he said urgently. I thrust the screwdriver at him and scrambled up the ladder.

"Look!"

I turned my head and peeped over the fence into the neighbor's backyard. Marching unsteadily up the back steps clutching the garden hose, was Siggy. An unbroken arc of water preceded him through the open door. As we watched, the small firefighter disappeared into the house.

"We've got to warn them!" I gasped.

"There's not time!"

"How far do you think Siggy will get?" I said fluctuating between horror and delight.

"Dunno, but I bet he is taking it into his bedroom."

As we spoke, our eyes fixated on the hose slithering along the ground and into the house.

"He's probably in the hallway by now," chuckled Ian gleefully. "Wait for it…"

A piercing scream rent the air.

"GET THAT THING OUT OF HERE! GARRRRY!"

"Pippa's seen it." We slid down the ladder and hid in the bushes, smothering our laughter like two naughty school kids.

"We could have tried harder to warn them," I said feeling guilty.

"There wasn't enough time."

"We should have yelled; it might have helped."

"But think of the fun we would have missed," sniggered Ian. We burst into silent laughter again. Ian parted the leaves and peered through the slats in the fence. I heard the squeaky noise of the outside tap being turned off in jerky movements.

"Does Gary look very wet?" I whispered.

"Can't see, his back is facing me, but his hair is dripping. We should go inside; he doesn't look in a good mood."

We crawled away from the fence and slid in the back door.

"It's time for a break anyway," I said putting on the kettle.

"Yeah, we'll carry on after a cuppa."

We had a leisurely break and then went back outside.

"All calm next door?" I said climbing up the wrong side of the ladder.

"Yip, pass me a thing-ummy-bob," said Ian climbing up the right side. "Let's see if I can get it in this time."

He positioned the chisel edge of the screwdriver carefully and pushed. The small point on the thing-ummy-bob buckled and sat down.

"YOU DOG!" Ian roared, flicking the useless thing onto the ground. "Give me another one he said through gritted teeth.

He concentrated hard and finally had success.

"Yahoo, you did it, that looks good," I clapped.

Ian smiled and wriggled another six triangles into the window frame. They stood at the bottom of the glass like the points of a tiny picket fence.

"You won't see them once we put a layer of putty over them," he said.

I was about to agree when something disturbing caught my eye.

"Hey Darls, I hate to mention this, but the top of the glass has popped out," I spoke nervously because it was the sort of message that got the messenger shot.

Ian blew hard through his nose and glared at me. His eyebrows jutted out and I saw signs of Vesuvius about to erupt.

"We might need to take everything out and try again.

Darling the Window is on Fire

I'll get the pliers to pull those thing-ummy-whatzits out," I quavered, scuttling away.

By the time I got back, Ian had cooled into lethargy. The calmness of defeat rested upon him.

"This is worse than the first time," he muttered as he repositioned the glass.

I stared at it sadly. He was right. Not only did we have putty oozing everywhere, the glass was completely smeared with greasy finger marks.

"We should have called a glazier," I said, my energy drooping like a wilted flower.

"You may be right." He drew his finger slowly through the grease. Like a filthy car, the impulse to write in the grime was irresistible. A head popped up over the fence.

"Are you having a spot of bother?" asked Gary. "I was mopping the porch when I saw your sign." He pointed to the large 'HELP' Ian had written on the window.

We eyed up Gary's delicate accountant's fingers doubtfully. "Fixing a window is not as easy as it looks," said Ian.

"I've had a bit of experience with glazing," said Gary. "Do you have a proper putty knife?"

Ian held up the butter-knife. "We've got this, it's near enough it has a rounded end."

"That won't do, I'll get mine and come over." Gary rummaged in the nearby shed and shortly after, vaulted over the fence.

"You've used too much putty; you only want a thin layer." He popped the greasy glass out, scooped away our efforts and expertly replaced them with a thin line of putty. "Now press the glass in like this and wriggle these little fellows in," he said demonstrating. "There you go. A bit more putty around the front, slide the excess off, and there you have it!"

Ian and I gazed at Gary in admiration, our respect for him soaring. The guy had lady's hands and knew nothing about heritage houses, but he sure knew how to fix a window.

"Thanks, mate that's great!" said Ian shaking his hand. "I heard you had a spot of bother yourself earlier."

"Yeah, Siggy took the hose inside and sprayed Pippa. She was reading the newspaper and enjoying a quiet smoke at the time. Didn't see him coming until the water hit her full in the face. The carpets sodden but it'll dry. It's the wallpaper we're worried about, the watermarks might be permanent," he said, his mouth drooping.

"Let me know if you decide to re-paper," I said to Gary. "Perhaps I could return the favor. I'm a dab hand at wallpapering."

"Sounds great." He waved and disappeared over the fence.

I thought of the cross-stitch on my bedroom wall. A red and a blue house stood next to each other above the words 'a good neighbor is a blessing.'

How true.

Planes, Kids and a Wardrobe.

In my opinion, my parent's beach house was the prettiest house Dad ever built. It was two stories with a steep roof and very cottagey. It nestled under Mount Mania, a range of almost sheer rocks that rose majestically into the sky. A short walk away was the sea; a glittering bright blue sea, stretching across a bay edged with white sand. One week, Ian went to Australia for a conference, and I took the opportunity to stay with Antoinette at the beach house.

"We saw Daddy get in a big plane and go up in the sky," said Marie, clutching her clown doll as we crunched up the gravel driveway.

"Did you honey," said Antoinette smiling.

"Thanks for letting me and the kids stay while Ian is away," I said carrying my suitcase inside. "It's nice to have a change of scene and a break from painting the house."

"No problem, I'm glad to have you to myself for a little while. How is the painting getting on?"

"Just about finished, I've only got the windowsills and the baseboards to paint. The dark green around the window architraves was a bit scary. The first coat made the house look like it had been punched in the eyes."

Antoinette giggled. "What did you do?"

"Carried on, two more coats made all the difference. The bruised look disappeared and now it's fabulous, every bit as good as the bungalow in Shortland Street.

"Who did the high area under the front gable?"

"Me. The height didn't worry me as much as the flex in the extension ladder. The top rungs bounce slightly as you climb. It gave me the willies when it moved. I'm relieved is over and done with."

"I know what you mean. I'm so glad to have the wallpaper up the stairwell finished."

"I bet. The steps and height make it difficult." I tilted my head back and scrutinized Antoinette's handiwork. "You've done a really good job, Mum and Dad will be pleased."

"I hope so."

"Do you like living at the beach?" I asked looking through the window at the kids swinging on the veranda railings.

"Yeah, it's great. It's a bit difficult without a car but I can catch the workers shuttle that goes in every day if I want to, and there is a good community here. I've got a group of regular customers who buy dolls and take doll-making classes."

"That's great. Do you find it a bit cramped with the shop in your living room?"

Antoinette pulled a face. "The open plan is challenging. The kitchen gets messy easily and dirty dishes are not professional."

Darling the Window is on Fire

"Mummy, Mummy, there's Daddy's plane!" said Marie rushing inside with Hannah in her wake.

"I think Daddy will be in Australia by now," I answered patiently, "that's a different plane."

"We saw Daddy get on a big plane," Hannah told Antoinette solemnly.

"Wow!" My sister pulled an astonished face. "How long is Daddy away for?"

Hannah stuck her finger in her mouth and stared dumbly, her powers of conversation exhausted by her single outburst.

"Three years," chirped her talkative sister.

Antoinette and I swapped smiles.

"The concept of years and days is confusing at that age," I said.

Another plane passed overhead.

"There's Daddy!" Marie shouted rushing outside to wave.

"I think Daddy is in Australia by ...oh forget it," I said as the door banged behind them. "What were we talking about?"

"The shop."

"Oh yeah, I've had a brainwave. Shift the shop upstairs. That big room is almost empty and the steep pitch of the ceiling is charming. Customers can go directly through the front door and up the stairs. If you keep this door shut," I pointed to the door at the side of the small entranceway, "all the bottom of the house would be private."

"Hmm, I like the idea of separating the house into a public and private area. But how would I fill that big room? I don't have enough stock?"

"Use the back area for your classes and have a theme. What about a Victorian Christmas? That goes well with porcelain dolls."

"But it's June!"

"So, what, celebrate Christmas all year," I said sweeping her objections aside. "It would be magical. You have a lovely tree, that looks realistic," I said, leading the way upstairs, "we could put it here," I spread my arms wide, "and you can borrow my clockwork train set. That would look cute around the base."

Antoinette's eyes sparkled as she caught the vision. "What about my antique wardrobe?"

"That would look stunning especially with your hat boxes on top. What else have you got?" I asked bustling back down the steps.

"There's my rocking chair?"

"Yeah, that would work. You could display dolls on it."

"Don't forget my antique horse bike."

"Oh yes, that thing is cool. The horse looks like a merry-go-round horse. It's bulky," I said eyeing up the large wheels of the Victorian tricycle as we walked past.

"Anything that fills a gap is good," said Antoinette.

"It will certainly fill a gap. A small child couldn't reach the peddles," I said skeptically, "I could ride it."

"I've got plenty of stuff we could use as props," said Antoinette moving on from the bike. "And heaps of Christmas decorations."

"Haul them out," I said excitedly.

"You are still a window-dresser at heart," laughed my sister as I followed her down two flights of stairs and into the garage.

"Never got that job out of my system," I agreed, "I love to set up displays and create an atmosphere." I hoisted up the roller door as I spoke.

"Mummy, Mummy, there's Daddy's plane." Marie burst through the door and pointed to a small white speck in the sky.

"Daddy is not on that plane. Daddy is in Australia by now," I explained patiently.

"Daddy's working on the plane," said Hannah looking at me with owl eyes.

"No, Daddy's not working on the plane. He's going to work in Australia."

"I can see Daddy," said Marie, waving frantically as she rushed back outside.

"They are not getting it, are they," said my sister.

"No, they're not. But at least it is keeping them entertained and out of our hair," I said through a gigantic armful of fake greenery. "Let's take everything upstairs and then we will shuffle it around to get the right effect."

For the next few hours, we worked at transforming the upstairs room into a Victorian wonderland.

"Time for lunch," said Antoinette at last. "I'm ready for a break."

"Me too. Perhaps a cup of tea will help us to work out how we are going to get that wardrobe up here," I said trailing down the stairs, "it weighs a ton."

"We could take the bottom drawer out," said Antoinette as she filled the kettle with water and cut sandwiches, "that would lighten it, it's solid oak and really heavy."

I went into her bedroom and pulled the bottom drawer out of the heavy piece of furniture.

"You're right," I called, as I upended it and emptied sweatshirts and jeans onto her bed. I swung open the door, scooped dresses from the closet and piled them beside the jeans. When it was completely empty, I lifted a side experimentally.

"This is still too heavy," I yelled down the hallway, "I tried lifting it and it is no go."

"That's a pain," my sister's voice floated back. I could hear her slicing tomatoes and the kettle whistling as I examined the hinges on the door.

"Have you got a Phillips screwdriver?" I called.

"Yeah." There were quick footsteps and Antoinette materialized carrying a red tool-kit. She dumped it on the floor and passed me a screwdriver.

"Hold this side of the door so it doesn't fall," I said, twisting the screw vigorously. "Here it comes."

"This is weighty," said Antoinette catching the door and dropping it onto the overloaded bed.

"But it is still too heavy," I said nudging the wardrobe. "Is lunch ready?"

"Yeah, let's eat. Food might give us inspiration. We have to get this upstairs, it's such a feature."

Marie burst through the door, Hannah following like the tail of a kite.

"Mummy, Mummy, I can see Daddy's plane!"

"That's nice," I said mechanically. "It's time for lunch." I handed them a plate of sandwiches each. "Don't drop crumbs on Auntie Antoinette's carpet. Either eat it in the kitchen or go outside again."

Another plane passed overhead.

"I can see Daddy," shouted Marie rushing outside with Hannah in her wake.

"Are they going to do this the whole time they are here?"

"Probably."

"That could get tiresome. I never realized how many planes pass each day."

"Not as tiresome as Marie yapping and Hannah helping," I reminded her.

"Oh, you are so right."

"What's happening with Sam, are you seeing him much?" I said changing the subject.

"He pops in from time to time," said Antoinette pouring tea into two cups. "Same old thing, he shows enough interest to keep me hoping, but not enough for me to be confident about him. I have no idea where I stand. I don't even know if we are going together or not."

"That is difficult," I said taking my tea and sandwiches, "at least your wedding dress is finished and packed away, remember how we had to hide it every time he came around."

"Yes," said Antoinette grimacing. She picked up her lunch and as if we were dragged by a magnet, we drifted into the bedroom and stared at the wardrobe. "He's like this thing," said Antoinette kicking the closet with her toe, "hard to move."

"That's a shame," I said absently. I stared into the empty wardrobe as I munched my sandwiches and finished my tea. Suddenly a brainwave hit me.

"Help me slide this out from the wall," I said dropping my plate, "I've had an idea."

"Ooo, that sounds interesting," said Antoinette drinking the last of her tea and whacking her cup down.

We took a side each and dragged it forward.

"As I thought," I exclaimed, rapping on the back. "This is tongue-and-groove. Each board is only held on with a couple of nails at either end. Where's your hammer?"

Antoinette flicked her toolbox open and handed me a hammer.

I slid the claw between the wood and the head of a small

nail and levered. The nail slid out easily.

"Piece of cake," I said whipping the remaining boards off.

"If this doesn't work, we are sunk. This is as far as we can go without destroying the whole thing," said Antoinette wrinkling her forehead.

"We'll soon find out. Take the other side and lift with your legs, not your back." We took a side each and heaved.

"Much better Wend."

"Yup, we can do this. Tilt it forward and I will catch the top, you take the bottom."

"Are you alright going backwards?" My sister's concern was touching.

"Yip, I usually end up carrying things backward, that's one area Ian is not chivalrous over, that and pillows. He always takes the best one."

We shuffled slowly out of the bedroom, down the small hallway, around a tight corner, through the kitchen, through the lounge, under the door lintel into the entranceway, and extra carefully around the sharp bend onto the staircase.

"Are you alright going up the stairs?"

"If we go slowly," I said feeling my way with my foot cautiously. "Tilt it more to get around the bend on the landing, that's it, just a bit more, done it." We staggered victoriously into the middle of the room.

"Marvelous," puffed Antoinette as we set our burden upright. We scooted downstairs, gathered up the discarded boards and hustled back up the steps.

Mummy, Mummy, shouted Marie rushing inside.

"We know, we know. You can see Daddy in the plane," Antoinette and I chorused together without breaking our stride.

"Yes," said Marie dashing back out again.

Putting the wardrobe back together was a small job.

"Nobody would guess we've nearly rebuilt this thing," I said, nailing the last board in place. I swung the closet door shut. "Look at that, it closes perfectly. Shove the bottom drawer in so we can get the full effect."

"Wow," said Antoinette stroking the carved tulip on a side panel. "It's a real feature all right. This room is amazing. Already it looks like Santa's grotto."

"Well, that's the goal." I climbed on a chair and knocked a small nail in the top of the closet. "What about hanging your jester here?" I hooked her string puppet over the nail so he dangled down the wardrobe.

"Wonderful, the red and green of his outfit looks fabulous against the timber."

"You'd better put a 'display only' sign on him if you don't want to sell him."

Antoinette shook her head vehemently. "I certainly don't want to sell him. I will never get another hand-carved puppet."

"Let's carry the counter up and start spreading the dolls and kit-sets around," I said climbing off the chair. "If we get the main stuff in place today, we can spend the next two days decorating,"

"Sure," said Antoinette sweeping a pile of Christmas ornaments to the side with her foot.

For the next few hours, we worked solidly.

"That is enough for a day," I groaned.

"My back is killing me," said Antoinette putting her hands in the small of her back and leaning backward.

"Me too," I said copying her. "I wonder what those kids are doing?"

Wendy Hamilton

"We haven't had any plane updates for a while," said Antoinette.

"No, we haven't, and it's gone suspiciously quiet," I said slowly. "I don't trust absolute silence. It's never golden. MARIE, HANNAH, WHAT ARE YOU DOING?"

"I'm making a surprise," called Marie from the garage.

"A surprise, that sounds ominous," I said to my sister as we hurried down the basement steps.

"I made Hannah into a clown," said Marie pointing at her handiwork with pride.

Our mouths dropped open and we gawped in dismay. The face-painting was horribly thorough. Bright pink cheek circles floated like life rafts on Hannah's sea-blue face. The victim sucked her thumb and stared happily at us through wide yellow rings around her eyes.

"She looks like my clown," said my irrepressible five-year-old holding up her clown doll. The statement was distressingly accurate. Hannah's enormous mouth and bright red nose made her a convincing clown.

"What is this stuff?" I said, scrubbing the blue chin with a damp cloth in vain. "It's not coming off!"

Antoinette examined a messy row of small jars nearby. "She has used my craft-paints." She handed me a bottle of turpentine. "I think they are oil based, try a bit of turps."

"It's still not coming off," I gasped. "Do you think we need to take her to the hospital?"

"How? The shuttle only goes once a day," quavered Antoinette. "We could try this?" She pulled a bottle from her first-aid-kit. "Hold still Honey."

A strong pungent smell filled the room as Antoinette scrubbed at Hannah's face. I held my breath fearfully.

"I think that eucalyptus oil is working," I said letting out a long sigh, as a small patch of skin appeared. "Don't ever do that again Marie that was very naughty!"

"I made Hannah pretty like my clown," said Marie unrepentantly. "Look there goes Daddy flying around in the plane!"

"Owww, that hurts, I wanna stay a clown!" Hannah's howls drowned out the sound of the overhead jet engines.

Lucky man, I thought glaring at the moving blob in the sky. I turned to my sister. "Maybe it is not such a bad thing if Sam is not interested. Why do you want to get married when it leads to this?" I grumbled, as together we scrubbed my daughter's bawling face.

I Told You So.

"You'll regret it," said Ian.

"It will be alright," I said naively, continuing to paint the house.

"You shouldn't let your mother drag you into this." He pointed to a thin patch, "you've missed a bit."

"I'm only going to have a look." I dabbed the offending spot. "Do you like this color?"

Ian gave it a casual glance. "It's alright. What time are they picking you up?"

"Six thirty, the evening service doesn't start until seven, but you know how they love to be early."

"I think your mother should leave it alone."

"Mum's biological clock is ticking for Antoinette," I said cutting in carefully around the veranda pillar. "Sam is only puddling around; he is not going to do anything. Mum had a dream. In the dream…" (I ignored Ian's snort) "a man from the West swooped in and carried off Antoinette." I stepped back and surveyed the baseboards with satisfaction. "That

Darling the Window is on Fire

red-brown gives the place a lift."

"What does that mean?"

"It means the colors zing."

"No, I'm talking about your mother."

"Oh, she thinks God has told her Sam won't marry Antoinette, but another man is coming quickly."

Ian raised his eyebrows in disbelief. "And now she knows who will marry Antoinette."

"Yeah, the chapel is west of the beach house and she has found," (I imitated my mother's voice) "a lovely little man who would be just right for the family. His name is Chris. Apparently, she and Dad have done their homework and his family background matches ours very well."

"That does not explain why you're going to have a look at him. Why doesn't she take Antoinette to church to meet him?"

"Haha, funny joke. You know perfectly well Mum cannot get Antoinette to do anything."

"As opposed to you, who she drags into all her schemes."

I gave him a hard look but held my peace. "Antoinette wouldn't marry superman if Mum and Dad suggested him."

"So, you are to suggest him."

I moved the paint bucket six steps to the left and started on the next set of baseboards.

"No, no, they just want to see what I think of him."

"You'll regret it and I'll say I told you so."

"No, you won't, because you won't get the chance. Everything will be fine."

"Yeah right! Just like your hair."

"What do you mean?

"It's full of paint. Have fun cleaning that out before you go tomorrow night."

Wendy Hamilton

The paint was out of my hair, and I was dressed in tidy clothes when Mum and Dad picked me up the following evening.

"Hello Dear," said Mum as I climbed in the backseat of the car. "Isn't this exciting?"

"Hello, I must admit I am curious to have a look at The Man."

"Well you will see him very soon," said Dad pulling out into a gap in the traffic.

So far so good. I thought as we arrived at the small brick church. Ian was being melodramatic predicting a dreadful evening. I crunched over the gravel carpark between Mum and Dad. This was the first time I had gone to their church. I noticed without surprise that most of the people filing in were elderly.

A stooped man stood at the door greeting people.

Mum patted his thin shoulder. "Hello Kevin, this is our daughter."

"Hello Antoinette, nice to have you with us," quavered Kevin, handing me a hymn book with gnarled hands. He looked at me curiously through faded eyes.

"No this is Wendy, our other daughter."

"I didn't know you had another daughter."

I took the book with growing discomfort, as the illusion of being single and unattached descended upon me like a Halloween costume. Suddenly I knew exactly why Antoinette would never have come. My discomfort was increased by all the stares. Newcomers were rare, as were eligible bachelors; there was only one. He was nearby checking the sound system.

"There's the little man," said Mum in a carrying stage whisper, "what do you think of him?"

Darling the Window is on Fire

"Shut up," I hissed frantically. Ian was right, this was a huge mistake. I wanted to shout, 'I'm the married daughter.'

Mum misinterpreted my distress. "He looks better from the front."

"It's hard to tell by looking at the back of his head," said Dad, also completely missing it.

"Shut up, shut up," I hissed, hustling them to the pew furthest away from Chris.

"Have you met him before," said Dad, looking disturbed by my reaction. "Is there a problem with him?"

By now both my parents were alarmed. They sat on either side of me and badgered me with questions. In her agitation, Mum forgot to whisper. It was unfortunate that the organ stopped playing right then. In the small gap of silence, her voice rang out loudly.

"Don't you think he's the one?"

For the rest of the evening, I fluctuated between blushes and mortification. In this instance, Ian was a true prophet. And he was merciless at rubbing my nose in it when I got home.

"OK. you can stop laughing now," I said, crawling into bed. "It wasn't funny. I've admitted to you twice that you were right and I'm not saying it again. It has been a long and mortifying evening, and I want to turn off the light and go to sleep."

"Just tell me the highlights one more time Wend so I can savor my victory," said Ian getting in his side.

"I will not, you've already heard everything three times. Your ego is big enough without me pandering to it."

Ian merely laughed louder.

I held my silence as long as I could.

"The worst part was that Mum had told half the

congregation she had a thirty-year-old unmarried daughter," I burst out, cringing all over again. "I'm sure the entire church heard her ask me what I thought of Chris as we passed him. I was glad he was busy with sound equipment and had his back to us. He can't have missed it, however. Nobody could have missed it. I was so embarrassed, which made it all the worse. I looked like their blushing unmarried daughter."

"Ha ha ha," gloated Ian.

"Mum kept asking me over and over, what do you think of The-Little-Man? And I kept telling her to shut up."

"I wish I'd heard you tell your mother to shut up. That must be a first."

"I was desperate."

"So, Antoinette has your total sympathy for non-cooperation?"

"Absolutely," I said, turning out the light.

A little over a week later, I had a visit from my parents. I was painting the house as usual when they arrived.

"Hello Dear, the house looks great," said my mother coming through the gate.

"Hello, Mum and Dad."

"Perhaps we should paint the beach house that color. What do you think Harold?"

"That would work," said Dad pulling the gate shut behind him. "It would go with the dark green roof."

"Yes, it would. What do they call that green?"

"Sweet Marjoram, I'll write it down for you. It's in the heritage section of the paint chart. Are you coming in for a cuppa?"

"Yes, that would be lovely. We have," (Mum paused and raised her eyebrows) "news."

"Oh, that sounds interesting," I said wrapping my

Darling the Window is on Fire

paintbrush tightly in a plastic bag so it would not dry out.

"It certainly is," said Dad as they followed me inside.

"What is this big news?" I asked once we were settled with tea around the table.

"Your father (a wonderful man) went up to Chris after church yesterday. Harold, tell Wendy what you said."

"I said to Chris, I have a thirty-year-old daughter,"

"Chris is thirty," interposed Mum.

"Who would kill me if she knew what I was doing," continued Dad. "She is short,"

"That's important because he is short…"

My father gave my mother a hard, quelling look. When Mum was sufficiently quelled, he carried on.

"If she entered Miss Northland nobody would laugh. Now the question is, if she is that good, why is she still available? The answer is that she is waiting for God's man and I think you might be him. Here is a map to her house. Her name is Antoinette and she has a doll shop in her home. Go in and buy a cheap doll for your niece if necessary."

"He has got a four-year-old niece. His sister is a lovely woman, three little children, two boys and…"

"Mother, I was speaking."

"Carry on."

"Buy a cheap doll if necessary, the Holy Spirit will tell you if she is right or not. If she is not, go away and she will never know anything about it. If she is right, ask her out."

"What did he say?" I asked agog.

"Not much just took the map."

"But we went around to his parent's place for lunch, and prayed together with them about it," finished Mum.

"Do you think Chris will go?" Ian asked me after I had repeated the conversation to him later that evening.

"Who knows? Dad's speech was bazaar."

Ian rubbed his nose thoughtfully. "Chris must at least be curious."

"I wonder if he will have the courage. Mum says he holds down a good job and has a house, moreover, he has never had a girlfriend which is good."

"Probably too busy getting other parts of his life together," said Ian.

I nodded. "He is nice looking, so it is not as if he couldn't have had one. One thing I am sure of however, he hasn't gone to see Antoinette yet."

"How do you know?

"She would have told me if he had."

"That's true."

Several days later, very early in the morning, Antoinette stalked into the kitchen wearing her haughty face.

"Did Mum and Dad send a man to see me?"

My heart sank, her tone was uppity. I hated it when she went all ice-maiden.

"Hello, you're early," I said, stalling. "You've just missed Ian."

"Tell me the truth." My sister's tone was cold and her eyes bored into me. "Did Mum and Dad send a man?"

There was a big pause while I scrabbled hopelessly for some way to slide out of the question.

"Did Mum and Dad send a Man?" She spoke slowly and pointedly.

"They might have."

"I knew it!" she exclaimed, her neck going stiff with annoyance. "I had something strange happen yesterday."

"Sit down and tell me about it," I said in a placating tone as I scooped the cat off the rocking chair by the woodstove.

Darling the Window is on Fire

"Have you had any breakfast?"

"I'm fine," she said taking the vacated chair with outraged dignity. "It was strange," she repeated. "I had my doll-class ladies around for a mid-winter-Christmas. We were downstairs in the lounge when a young man arrived and wanted to see around the shop. I took him upstairs and he stayed for ages. So long, I got worried about the turkey in the oven."

"Oh dear, that is distressing," I soothed, pulling another chair up the fire and sitting down. "It would be terrible to burn a turkey."

Antoinette ignored my interruption. "He circled aimlessly and eventually bought a doll." "I kept wishing he would go, right up to the end..."

"What happened at the end?" I asked agog with curiosity.

My sister's neck softened and she relaxed her rigid posture. "He smiled. He has a lovely smile." Her uppity tone melted into friendliness. "It lit up his whole face. I was so blown away I nearly wrote on the back of his check, ask me out. Wasn't that odd?"

I nodded. "Very odd."

"I thought about it all night," (her neck stiffened again) "and the more I thought about it, the more I was sure Mum and Dad were behind it. Now I know I am right; I'm not interested in him." She stamped her foot as her face slid into haughtiness.

"Not even someone with a nice smile?"

"He did have a lovely smile." Her neck and eyes softened momentarily. "But he is not my type," she said going rigid. "He is too quiet…"

"Come and talk to me while I paint, I have nearly finished," I said, changing the subject as I lead my fuming sister outside. "Tell me what you think about the colors."

"Yeah, it looks good." Without looking she sat down on the front steps.

"I can't wait to start on the shingles under the bow window," I said, opening a bucket of paint and stirring. "Painting those will make a big difference."

"I cornt imagine him yachting," said Antoinette in her posh voice.

"The red-brown will balance the brown shingles under the veranda rail on the other side," I said in my normal voice.

"I don't think he would fit in with the hospital crowd," my sister continued speaking with a plum in her mouth.

"Mum is thinking of painting the beach house Sweet Marjoram."

"Don't speak of my interfering parents! Anger killed the English accent.

"It is hard to get paint out of hair," I said hoping to distract her attention.

"Huh, you get off lightly. I'd rather have paint than parents in my hair. Can you imagine how embarrassing, going with them to meet a man would be?"

"Yes, I certainly can!"

"Only a fool would go."

Ian's gloating face loomed into my mind and his words echoed in my brain. "I told you so."

I nodded. "Only a fool would go," I agreed.

Unexpected Possibilities.

Ian and I took an end each of a wooden trestle and lifted. "I'm so glad the painting is finished and it is the weekend again," I said, "it's the bright spot in my week."

"Most people feel that way."

"The kids are driving me crazy. See that," I jerked my head towards a huge mark on the garage floor, "Yesterday Marie spilled the paint, while Hannah gave the cat a haircut."

The light of understanding broke over Ian's face. "So that's why he looks so motley."

"And they trash their bedroom as soon as my back is turned."

"Ah huh, is that so." Together we shuffled out the garage door.

"Marie talks incessantly and nearly poisoned Hannah. Thank goodness she didn't drink much! Some of those cleaning products are lethal."

We maneuvered the gangling trestle through the tiny

entry around into the kitchen. "That kiddy-lock was supposed to be child-proof," said Ian.

I shuffled forward awkwardly. "It certainly wasn't Marie-proof. You know how we wanted four children?"

"Yes."

We doe-see-doed around the door into the hallway. "I've really gone off the idea," I said as we swung into the lounge. "Motherhood is hard."

Ian put his end down and lifted my end upright. "We can stop at two if you want."

I nodded. "Great, two is more than enough," I said watching him spread the trestle into a ladder.

Now we had solved that problem, I lifted my eyes to the ceiling. "I can't wait to see all the paint off those beams. I am glad the paneling in the entrance is original."

"So am I. I wish they'd left the window-seat unpainted."

"Good thing you have had plenty of practice stripping the kitchen."

"Huh, I hope I am not going to remove all the paint and then have you say," (Ian's voice rose to a high falsetto) "I don't like it, paint it again."

I pulled a face at him. "You're quite safe, I love natural timber. And it is only four beams."

"It's more than four beams. It's also skirtings, architraves, and doors. You get the easy part."

"I know, but finishing the fiddly bits is hard work too." I looked at the beams spread across the ceiling. "It looks like a noughts and crosses game."

Ian grinned and shot me a sideways glance. "I could paint circles and Xs in the spaces between the beams?"

"Don't you dare! Your graffiti on the back wall was bad enough!

Darling the Window is on Fire

We walked out to the garage, grabbed another trestle and shuffled back inside.

"I had an interesting conversation with a guy from Waikato University yesterday," said Ian changing the subject as he stepped over a plank lying on the floor.

"Did you?"

We dumped our burden opposite the first trestle.

"He suggested I go to University." We picked up the plank and Ian slid his end onto the trestle nearest him.

"University!" I shoved my end onto the one closest to me. "Why?"

"He suggested I do a Master's degree in Materials Science."

"But you don't have a Bachelor's degree?"

"My qualifications and experience make me eligible. It would be an advantage. There is a prejudice against Technical College qualifications."

I leaned weakly against the trestle. "How could we afford it?"

"I talked to my boss and the company will fund it. We have to live in Hamilton for ten months, but I can finish the rest by correspondence. If we got tenants, we could afford to rent a house."

"Hmm." I imagined myself walking down the main street of Hamilton. "A change of scene might be fun."

Ian nodded. "I think so."

I picked up a tarpaulin. "Lift the trestle," I said.

Ian lifted the legs one by one and I pushed the tarpaulin under them. The telephone rang just as we finished.

"Hello," I said into the bulky receiver.

"Hello Wend."

"It's Antoinette," I mouthed to Ian as Antoinette talked.

Wendy Hamilton

"You're what?" I sank into a nearby armchair.

"I'm going out with Chris," my sister repeated calmly.

"Antoinette is going out with Chris," I hissed up at Ian. He had climbed onto the plank and was scraping at the beams.

"How did that happen? It's six weeks since Dad talked to him. I thought he was not interested."

"Me too, and if he had come any sooner, I would have told him to get lost."

Paint flakes cascaded down and settled in my hair. "Hold on a minute, I need to move. Ian is stripping the beams in the lounge and I am getting covered in dust." I put the phone down and dragged my chair away from the trestles. "OK go on, I'm all ears."

"I got so lonely, I wished someone doing a political survey would knock on the door."

"That's desperation!"

High above me, beautiful dark beams were emerging as Ian worked. I caught his eye and twisted my thumb up like a cat's tail.

"There was a knock on my door," continued my sister, "and Chris stood there saying nothing until it got a little awkward, so I said, did my parents send you? He nodded and I invited him in. It was uncomfortable until my mechanical doll saved the day."

"What mechanical doll?"

"You know, the clockwork one."

"Oh, yeah, how's that coming on?"

"It's good now, but I was having trouble with the arms on Saturday, the mechanism kept jamming. It turns out, amazing things happen if you put an ex-watchmaker and an engineer together, with a mechanical problem. We worked on that doll all afternoon. Before he left, he invited me to a Christmas party and I accepted."

"Really?"

"Yes really. We went last night and it was hilarious."

"Antoinette went out with Chris last night!" I mouthed to Ian.

"It was a Faulty Towers evening."

"Faulty Towers. Isn't that a British comedy?" I raised my eyebrows at Ian.

"That's right."

"I've never seen the program but I've heard it is a hotel where everything goes wrong."

"Exactly! To begin with, the key was lost and we had to enter the hotel by climbing in the window. Then all the guys without a girl had to sing a solo. The whole evening was a crack up. We laughed and laughed."

"It sounds like a fabulous icebreaker."

"Yeah, it was, on the bus home I could have kissed the man."

"Did you?"

"No of course not, that is too fast. Any-hoo," (Antoinette's voice went all kittenish) "end of the story is that Chris and I are going out."

My eyes popped and my mouth dropped open. "Do Mum and Dad know?"

"Heck no!" The British accent burst forth dripping with haughtiness. "I've sworn him to secrecy. I told him he wouldn't know what hit him if they got involved."

"That's a bit harsh don't you think?"

Britain disappeared and she spoke brusquely. "Well, that's the way I see it. Don't you tell them. Promise?"

"Oh all right."

Wendy Hamilton

We talked a little longer and then I hung up.

"So, your sister is going out with Chris."

"Yeah." I scrutinized the ceiling. "I am loving what you're doing, those beams look amazing."

"The timber is really nice," agreed Ian pulling down his dust mask.

"I can't believe how much lower the ceiling looks. It alters the room dramatically. Why would anyone paint all the character out?"

"Beats me. Tell me about Antoinette and Chris," he said climbing down the trestle.

"Did you get that Chris went around last Saturday?"

"Yeah," he said brushing paint flakes off his overalls before sinking into an armchair.

"You know that mechanical doll Antoinette was making? They worked on it together all afternoon." I recounted the conversation blow by blow.

When I had finished Ian stood up. "I hope our kids don't turn out like your sister. She doesn't honor your parents much." He walked over to a trestle and nudged it across the room.

"No, she doesn't. She speaks as if she was abused," I agreed, mirroring his action with the other trestle.

"Where does she get those silly ideas from?"

"Her head. As a child, she had difficulty separating fact from fantasy."

We lined the trestles up under the next beam. "She still does," said Ian.

I pulled the tarpaulin into the new position. "When it comes to Mum and Dad she does, they are not perfect but they are extremely caring. Chris will think they are monsters."

Darling the Window is on Fire

Ian pushed an armchair into the hallway. "Yet they are great in-laws. Your mother hacks me off from time to time but she is a good egg."

"It looks like big changes are coming," I said as we dragged the couch out of the way. "I wonder what next year will bring?"

"Who knows, life is full of surprises," said Ian clambering up and starting to scrape again. "You didn't expect a phone call like that this morning."

"Or the possibility of shifting to Hamilton," I said. "Do you think Antoinette will end up marrying Chris? Mum's sure it will happen."

"Your mother is sure about all sorts of things," snorted Ian. "She even thinks God has told her we are going to have two sons."

I clenched my teeth as I thought of the paint stain and the bald cat. "That is the only thing I'm certain about," I said emphatically. "We are definitely calling it quits at two girls."

Wendy Hamilton

Renovations can be Romantic.

We did go to Hamilton. While we were away, Antoinette got engaged to Chris, and I gave birth to a son.

"I can't wait to get home," I said to Ian, as I strapped our six-week-old baby into his car seat on the morning of our departure. "This has been a rest but there is no place like home."

"A rest! Maybe for you, I wouldn't call studying my eyeballs out a rest!"

"Having a baby is not restful either. I was referring to the house renovations. I haven't held a paintbrush or scraper in my hand for almost a year."

A wistful look crept into Ian's eyes and his mouth drooped. "I miss my wrecking bar. Unfortunately, there is not much more I can demolish."

"There is still all the carpet to rip up," I said cheerfully.

"Yeah," his face split into a wide grin as he turned to the girls, "do you need to go to the bathroom before we go?"

Darling the Window is on Fire

"No," Marie and Hannah chorused.

"It's going to be a long trip, are you sure?"

"Yes."

"Alright get in," he looked at me, "I'll lock up while you buckle them in."

"Can I have Oliver on my knee," asked Marie clambering over pillows and blankets.

"No, cats hate traveling. He's going in the cat carrier."

"He won't mind sitting on my knee."

"Yes, he will, as soon as the van starts, he'll hide under a seat."

Marie shook her head in disagreement. "He won't be able to. There's stuff under all of them." She had a point. Every available inch was crammed with luggage.

"I'm not having a loose cat in the van while Daddy is driving. It is not safe. Listen to his howling, he is not happy. If you promise to leave him in his cage, however, he can sit between you and Hannah." I swung the cat-carrier over Hannah and plunked it in the small gap between them. Then I slid the seat belt over Marie and clipped the buckle in place.

"I want my Santa bear," said Marie, as I buckled Hannah in safely.

"Here," I said passing her a soft toy. Marie scrutinized it closely.

"This is not my Santa Bear, it's Hannah's.

"They are exactly the same."

Her eyebrows lowered and her lips pouted. "No, my bear has a necklace. I want my bear."

I could see a patch of white fluff squashed against the glass of the rear door.

"Can't you make-do with Hannah's bear?" It was a futile hope.

Wendy Hamilton

"I want my Santa Bear, Marie's got my Santa bear," whined Hannah complicating matters.

"Oh, all right," I said giving in.

I squeezed the catch gently and gingerly lifted the hatch an inch. A small rubber-ball dropped to the ground and rolled past my feet. I waited until I was sure everything was stable and lifted the door slowly.

"Can you see Santa Bear?" Marie shouted.

I stretched out my hand carefully and spoke slowly. "I've almost got him."

"Oh, goodie." Marie gave a small bounce. Suddenly like a Jack-in-the-box, the luggage exploded. Three left shoes, two textbooks, a sippy-cup, four duvets, sixteen soft toys, a bag of baby clothes, and my sewing machine, cascaded to the ground.

"What did you do that for?" erupted Ian materializing at my side like lava from Pompeii.

I waved the Santa Bear in justification. "Marie wanted her Santa Bear. I think it will make the journey go smoother if she has something to play with. It is a long way."

"I spent all morning packing and repacking to get this door shut," he grumbled in a puff of temper. He rolled a duvet into a tight ball and wedged it between a suitcase and the left window.

"You are good at this. I could never pack so much in," I said admiringly. He paused, held a textbook aloft and surveyed his handiwork with satisfaction. We both knew I spoke the truth and the volcano went dormant.

"You go next door and give the key back to the landlord," he said in a modified tone. "I'll have this repacked by the time you get back."

True to his word we pulled out of the driveway exactly

Darling the Window is on Fire

as he predicted. And six hours later we drove down our own driveway.

"That was a long trip," I said, as I carried the baby onto the back porch. The girls, crumpled and grizzly, trailed behind. "Traveling with kids is hard work. I'm glad to be home."

"There is no place like home," nodded Ian unlocking the back door.

Peace and comfort engulfed me as we trooped into the kitchen. The girls, seeing familiar surroundings, perked up. They ran through the house squealing.

I picked a welcome-home card off the bench. "Nice of Antoinette and Chris to set everything up for us, especially their wedding so close. I thought we would have to unpack the backroom as soon as we got home."

Ian nodded. "Antoinette has done a good job remembering where everything goes."

"Yes, she has, it's lucky the sunroom is lockable. I don't know what we would have done without it."

"It has worked out well." Ian scanned the room rapidly. "The tenants have left everything as they found it."

I put the card down. "I hope they are enjoying their new house.

"The builders got it finished just in time," said Ian as we wandered slowly through all the rooms soaking up the atmosphere. That atmosphere was what made this modest house extraordinary. It was not a haunted house. There was no ghost. A presence, however, dwelt in it. It was as if the house had a soul. Either that or it was filled with angels or the hem of God's robe.

"This is your new home Joe," I said to the baby as I introduced him to the house.

Wendy Hamilton

"I can't believe how much character this place has," said Ian as we completed the circuit by returning to the kitchen. "When you live with it all the time it is easy to take it for granted."

"I know what you mean. Of course, ten months in a shoe box heightens the effect."

A loud 'hellooooo' sounded from the backdoor.

"COME IN."

There was a clatter in the back entranceway and Antoinette popped through the kitchen door. Chris followed in her wake.

"Hello," I said, rushing to give her a hug. "Welcome to the family Chris. Are you nervous about your wedding next Saturday?"

"He's a lucky man, he's getting me," Antoinette answered for him with a laugh and a quirky smile.

"Thanks for sorting all this out," I said pointing to the furniture.

"No problem. Repay me by bringing the girls around to my place for a dress fitting," said my sister pulling big smiley faces at her new nephew. "They will make sweet flower girls. And you can see the new house of course."

"I am longing to see it. Thanks for keeping me updated with all your letters. I have been wondering what to get you as a house-warming present."

"Don't worry about it. Chris and I had so much stuff between us, we had to have a garage sale. Even though it is a huge house, there was not room for everything."

"That is a first, most couples struggle to get furniture, let alone buy a house."

My sister waved her hands airily. "One of the advantages of getting married later. We don't need to scrimp. Come and

Darling the Window is on Fire

see it as soon as you get settled. The cats and I are in sole possession until the honeymoon." She giggled. "Poor Chris, he bought it but I get to live in it."

"I wouldn't have it any other way," smiled Chris.

It did not take long to settle back into a routine. A few days later I went to see Antoinette's new house. It stood at the side of a very busy road, and as I expected, was beautiful and imposing. It was built at the turn of the twentieth century and iced like a wedding cake, with gables and fretwork, verandas and bay-windows.

I sucked in my breath and clapped my hands together as Antoinette welcomed me into the wide entranceway. "I love your house."

"It is good isn't it, I'll give you a tour."

I was relieved that she was in a friendly mood. I loved it when she was warm. We scampered about the house like kids, exploring all the nooks and crannies. When I'd seen everything, we settled down to the important business of fitting the girl's dresses.

Marie stood on a stool wearing her wedding clothes. "Good choice," I said. "The dark tartan and navy silk look so good together. Classic styles always look smart.

Antoinette's lips bristled with pins. "I wanted a timeless style," she murmured out of the corner of her mouth. Marie wriggled. "Hold on sweetie or you will get a pin stuck in you," She stepped back and squinted at the bottom of the dress. "I think the hem looks better that height."

"It does," I said pinning my side of the hem.

"Chris and I are hiring a vintage car for the wedding. It will go with the era of the house and look good in photos. I'll put our wedding picture over the fireplace," she said pointing at a spot on the wall.

Wendy Hamilton

"This really is a lovely house," I said gazing around. I remembered her derogatory remarks about my house, and could not resist adding, "I am surprised, however, by some of its features. I recall you hated verandas.

"Only little verandas like yours," said Antoinette. "My veranda is a return veranda." She stressed the word 'return' in the Queen's accent and remained British for the rest of the conversation. "Return verandas swoop around the corner and give graciousness to a large villa like this. I always thought your house was a big house," (that was news to me) "but now I realize it is really rather small." (My worldview returned to normal.)

A big truck rumbled past the front window, rattling the teacups in the china cabinet.

"Doesn't the heavy traffic bother you? I remember you said you could never live on a main road. We get lots of cars but the trucks have to take the bypass."

"It would worry me if my house was as close to the road as yours is." The teacups tittered again as a cattle-truck ground up the hill in low gear. "I always wanted a manor with grounds," she said, sweeping her hand towards the scraggly boundary hedge. I looked at the empty patch of grass. The way she talked made it hard to believe there were no fountains, knot-gardens or lavender beds.

"Does the house get much sun? I asked naughtily.

"No," admitted my sister.

"But you said you couldn't live in a house that wasn't streaming with sun."

"When you have furnishings like mine, sun is overrated. The New Zealand sun is so harsh on fabric."

The cat walked in.

"Why is Boston wearing a sweater?"

Darling the Window is on Fire

A happy day.

Wendy Hamilton

Antoinette giggled and her voice returned to normal. "He got so cold I had to knit him one. These old villas are beautiful but they are freezing."

I picked Boston up and patted him on the head. "Did you have much trouble getting it on him?"

"He fussed of course, but eventually he gave in. Siamese cats feel the cold. I have to wear two pairs of socks to bed and it is not even winter."

"Me too, old houses are hard to heat. I have seriously thought of making a nightcap to keep my head warm. Four-poster beds were probably invented for practical reasons. The curtains and canopy would keep the warmth in."

It was a mistake to mention four-poster-beds.

Antoinette's eyes glazed over. "A four-poster bed, now that's an idea I could get into." Although she still spoke in her native accent, her top lip was elongating. I did not want the closeness of the moment ruined by Britain again.

"So Mum was right about Chris after all," I said hastily.

"I guess so."

I could not have chosen a better subject to wipe haughty off her face.

"Are we finished yet?" whined Marie shuffling with impatience.

"Yes. You can take the dress off and put your clothes back on," Antoinette said helping her off the wooden stool.

"When did you tell Mum and Dad?" I asked as Marie scampered away.

"Just before we got engaged. I said, Mum and Dad, I have something to tell you. They looked at me nervously and I said, I have been going out with Chris for six months. Mum said, who is Chris? And I said, you know, Christoper from church. Then Mum danced around the room screaming

Darling the Window is on Fire

with joy."

I smiled, visualizing the scene. "That sounds like Mum,"

Antoinette stiffened and my old enemy Haughty Face was back.

"That sort of ghastly behavior is exactly why I didn't tell them sooner," said the family princess through her nose. "Chris wanted to ask Dad if he could marry me," but I said, (princess melted into peasant) "yeah right as if he would say no! They did, after all, pick you."

"I guess you have an arranged marriage." The idea was amusing.

"I suppose so," admitted Antoinette shuddering. "Don't make a big deal of it. I don't want Mum and Dad's success to go to their heads."

I laughed. "Well, you do have Mum and Dad to thank for the fact that very soon you will be Mrs. Chris. Where are you going for your honeymoon, or is that a secret?"

"Chris's got three weeks off work. We are touring the South Island for two weeks." The 'face' and Britain resurfaced. "I want to see Larnachs Castle. But the last week…" (her voice returned to normal) "we are painting the kitchen. I can't live with this color." She fiddled with a hammer absentmindedly.

"It is foul," I agreed, grimacing. "I hate hot pink."

She pointed to an architectural defect. "So is that." As she spoke, the family DNA pulled Antoinette's face and voice back to normal. "And we will demolish that wall. It is obviously an addition and not built to code."

I beamed with pleasure. My sister was loveable when she had a hammer in her hand.

"If you haven't bought us a wedding present yet Wend, I'd like a circular saw," she said humbly. "We need it for our honeymoon."

"I can't think of a better way to start a marriage," I said thinking fondly of Ian. Shared projects build relationships. When you are best friends, even house renovations are romantic.

About the Author

Wendy Hamilton resides in Australia with her husband Ian and her four children. Wendy enjoys crafts, gardening, writing and drawing.

Wendy Hamilton

Other Books By Wendy Hamilton

<u>Eating a Light Bulb Does Not Make You Bright</u>
Light on Home-Schooling

<u>I told you not to Climb the Cactus.</u>
Surviving the Badlands of Motherhood

Children's Novels
<u>The Britwhistles win a Prize</u>
<u>The Britwhistles and the Elasticizer</u>

Children's Picture books
<u>The Unlucky Snails</u>
<u>The Unlucky Snails go to France</u>

These can be found at
www.zealauspublishing.com

www.ingramcontent.com/pod-product-compliance
Lightning Source LLC
Chambersburg PA
CBHW021105080526
44587CB00010B/391